GIFTS OF THE SPIRIT

True Stories to Renew the Soul

GIFTS OF THE SPIRIT

True Stories to Renew the Soul

By *Ardath Rodale*

Photographs by Anthony Rodale

Daybreak™ Books
An Imprint of Rodale Books
New York, New York

Daybreak is an imprint of Rodale Press, Inc.

Printed in Hong Kong on acid-free (∞), recycled paper ♻

Cover Designer: Barbara Scott-Goodman
Cover Photographer: Anthony Rodale

Library of Congress Cataloging-in-Publication Data
Rodale, Ardath H.
 Gifts of the Spirit: true stories to renew the soul / by Ardath Rodale:
 photographs by Anthony Rodale.
  p.   cm.
  ISBN 0–87596–487–7 hardcover
  1. Spiritual life—Christianity. I. Title
  BV4501.2.R6197 1997
  242—dc21   97-6590

Distributed in the book trade by St. Martin's Press

2 4 6 8 10 9 7 5 3 1 hardcover

──────── OUR PURPOSE ────────

"*We publish books that empower
people's minds and spirits.*"

DAYBREAK

To all the special angels in heaven
and those here on earth

CONTENTS

Chapter 5: Health 54

Chapter 6: Love 64

Chapter 7: Nature 76

Chapter 8: Quiet Self 88

Chapter 9: Gratitude 96

ACKNOWLEDGMENTS

I thank all the special people who were there to encourage
and inspire me for *Gifts of the Spirit*.

I send bouquets of appreciation to:
• Anthony Rodale, for his extreme sensitivity in seeing life through photography.
• My family, for being there with their care.
• My grandchildren and day care children, who keep me young in spirit.
• Michele Horon, my assistant and friend, who gives me
valuable feedback. She is a sounding board and springboard for
many new ideas.
• Dana Grim, my niece, who helped me heal.
• Mike Krajsa, a friend who encourages me to grow.
• The Mennonite families surrounding me, who remind me to remember
life in its simplicity.
• Karen Kelly, my editor, who is a pleasure to work with.
• Jane Colby Knutila and Barbara Scott-Goodman, who were instrumental
in the design and layout of the book.
• All the other members of the team who helped bring this project together:
Kelly Bogh, Helen Clogston, and Kathy Everleth.

I am especially grateful to be alive in this beautiful world, and grateful to
all those who have enriched my life. I circle all with love...

INTRODUCTION

Keep a few embers
From the fire
That used to burn in your village
Some day go back
So all can gather again
And rekindle a new flame
For a new life in a changed world

DAKOTA INDIANS

Storytelling

As a child, I would return each day from school and share with my family what I had learned. I had a strong need to offer them my constant amazement at my life's daily discoveries.

Later on, to keep my children occupied on trips, these real-life experiences became "story time." There were two sets of children with a six-year difference between, so these stories became duplicated. The older children teased me by giving the stories they'd already heard numbers.

Still later, after my mother died, I acquired all the family pictures of old relatives. There were many copies, so finally I asked my brothers and sister to come and choose which pictures they would like to keep. As we looked through the photographs, the lives of these people became real as I told stories related to the people in the photographs. My siblings looked at me in astonishment and asked, "How do you know all this stuff?" I replied, "I asked."

I've been pondering life changes with the generations and asking, "With television, computers, and busy family schedules, what kind of family history do parents teach? Do our children know their roots, where they came from, and who they are?" Their lives need to be touched not only by the new, but by the living hearts of those people who came before. It's vitally important to study new things but also to remember what we can learn from the past. I believe we are entering a new age where people will begin to have another look at their roots as a way of surviving in a world where we are moving too fast. Indigenous people are teaching us about gifts we didn't know we had.

My son and I are collecting African art. Recently, we purchased a wooden life-size sculpture of a man. This sad-looking native with his hands on his knees sat for more than 130 years in the middle of a village in Mali. He represented a storyteller and was a symbol of the villagers' heritage.

Storyteller now sits in my home office. You can feel his vibrations in the room; he is a silent reminder of the gifts we have to give each other. They are gifts of ourselves and our spirits that enhance the essence of our everyday lives.

Please join me on this journey.

Balance and Harmony

Everything in life is so delicate,
it's a matter of balance.

BILL ZIMMERMAN

WEAVING
LIFE'S DESIGN

Do you realize that every day you pick up the threads of your life to weave them together? Sometimes our colors are bright and cheerful while at other times they are dark and somber. We weave not only our colors but also those of family, friends, co-workers, and others in the community with whom we interact. What happens in their lives is stitched into the same fabric as our lives. We are all woven together.

There is a special kind of weaving called double weaving in which a different pattern is woven on each side of the cloth, producing a wonderful work of art. It reminds me not only of how *we* feel when we face challenges but also how other people react to that experience.

A good example of this is what happens in a family when parents and children often don't realize that both are facing different situations at the same time. Each person is only concentrating on their own concerns when what they really need is to share what is going on in each other's lives and look for solutions together.

That is how to weave the family masterpiece. We need to raise each other up and let both parents and children realize that they have value. Each person is a bright thread to be treated with respect and dignity.

Once, when I was facing a hard situation in my family, I asked our Mennonite neighbor how she dealt with difficult struggles in her family, and she said to me, "Ardie, you just let them know that you love them all the while."

The human spirit strives for wholeness. We need to look at life as a tapestry, a unified society to which we each contribute. I can't help but think of a wonderful analogy from grade school. It was May Day, a day of dance and celebration. At the culmination of the program was the Maypole dance. Ribbons were attached to a high pole. Each person took the end of a ribbon, and as they stretched out we became like the spokes of a wheel. As the music progressed, the dancers wove in and out in an intricate design around the center of the pole.

In our lives, the many spokes of experience and interaction among us makes the wheel stronger as we come closer together in harmony. The wheel is the weaving of our world into one.

Close your eyes for a moment to think about the life you are weaving. What do you see? It continues to grow as long as you live. *You* choose the colors! *You* can pick those bright golden threads that enrich the whole pattern.

THE MUSIC OF OUR LIVES

In my living room I have a Celtic harp that fascinated two of my grandsons. They were eager to learn how to tune it so they could play it, and tuning became a group effort. One child pressed the designated piano key and the other child pressed the foot pedal as I tightened each string on the harp and asked them to tell me when they heard the two tones resonating as one. "Yes, yes, we hear it! It's magic!"

This was not only a lesson in tuning an instrument; it also illustrated a valuable life lesson: In order to play beautiful music, we need to continually fine-tune our bodies so all parts of us play harmoniously together.

Think what happens when all the instruments in an orchestra play in harmony—a masterpiece is created not just by one, but by a community of players. Our community of players is all those people who touch our lives. As we come together, we are learning not only to develop a talent for getting along with one another but also to help bring joy to each other. Looking back to the Old Testament, David soothed King Saul's disturbed mind by playing his harp. Recently, I've been reading that music is enjoying a resurgence as therapy for people with many kinds of illnesses. Music can touch the sensitivity of our souls to heal our emotions and spirits. Has music touched your life in this way?

Some of us will never master an instrument, but we can learn to master appreciation. In my teen years I enjoyed playing the violin in the school orchestra. Now when I hear a virtuoso playing magnificently, I become that artist in my mind. My fingers move nimbly over the strings as the bow glides tenderly, creating music to warm my heart and surround me with love and peace.

I am often alone now as many of us are these days. Coming home from work, sometimes filled with tension from the events of the day, I prepare a simple meal, and music becomes my companion throughout a candlelight dinner. The music serves as a transition from the pressures of the day, and as calmness envelopes me, I am able to relax and be ready to greet a new day.

The music of the outdoors can be some of the most beautiful music of all. Nature sings to you as you hear the birds and listen to the rustle of the grass on a dewy morning. Even the distant sound of a train whistle or the crunch of snow beneath your feet or the laughter of children can add to life's symphony. All these wonders of nature are yours to hold sacred as precious jewels.

Music can wrap around you like a warm blanket to give you a feeling of love and peace, or it can fill you with unbounded energy to release built-up stress.

Just look at the potential for each one of us to create music and healing in our lives: to interpret, to appreciate, to share. Let your mind become inspired, your body stretched with energy, and your spirit touched with love. Listen to—and play—the music of your life! Aren't we rich?

MOVING
TOWARD HARMONY

I was a bundle of nerves as I left for a long-overdue vacation. Part of the reason was that I have difficulty leaving home unless the slate is clean. If you are like I am, it's difficult to close the door and just let go.

As part of the vacation, I learned a valuable lesson. Early every morning, the 11 women who were part of the group I traveled with came together in silence. The outdoors was our stage. We opened our arms to honor the sky and earth as we brought this energy together to remember that Nature is our teacher. We opened the curtain of our busy lives to bring in expanded wonder and awareness of the treasures that surrounded us. We were participating in the ancient art of tai chi. It is the practice of fluid movements that can teach us to stay centered in our lives. This is one of the greatest gifts we can give ourselves.

I thought about why this is so important. When storms and challenges face us in life, our breathing shallows and the feeling of exhaustion takes control. In our daily encounters we need to remember to reduce that tension by breathing deeply. Knees need to remain soft so that we can bend like the branches of the trees, which sway with the elements but which will always come back to their centers.

As the week wore on, each day the tension lessened, and on the last morning of vacation, as we sat listening to some special thoughts after the tai chi session, I marveled as I saw a miracle. I saw the grass not as a green carpet but as a breathing wonder of trillions of moving, tiny green blades of different varieties of grass. Was it the gentle breeze, or an ant crawling to its destination, or the springing back from the weight of my boot that caused all this motion? Tai chi was speaking through me to say, "Face the light of all the wonder surrounding you. This is the path to health and joy. Remember that this can only happen when you stay centered. By breathing deeply, you become the receptacle for the amazing oneness of all life."

Then I thought about the relationship among the earth, the sky, and ourselves.

I believe that the earth is the reality of all experience. The sky stands for the composite of all of our dreams, and as they are mixed together to surround us in our center, we become the vessel of calm and love, and harmonious energy is multiplied.

This is what I'm striving for. How about you?

FINDING THE JOYFUL BALANCE

Do you keep a "Have To" list? Most of the time we can tackle the easy tasks and cross them off with a flourish. Then, with a huge sigh, we realize that there still exist the remaining projects that we'd rather not do. This happened to me recently, the result of which I'd like to share with you. I think I will remember this experience forever.

My schedule was extremely busy, and in the midst of all that needed to be done, I had to go to Chicago to give a speech. I was so far behind that I still hadn't written my talk. Plus, I was filled with rebellious thoughts of why I shouldn't go and how I could make much better use of my time.

At the last minute, as I was ready to leave for the airport, I grabbed an inspirational mag-azine to read on the airplane. With a grum-bling mind, I read the words on the cover: "Work and Play: Finding the Sacred Balance."

As I read article after article, my mind began to relax. I stopped for a moment and looked at the panoramic Earth below and the powdery clouds surrounding me in the blue sea of sky. Peace filled me and one by one my neg-ative thoughts dropped like stones and disap-peared into nothingness. Slowly, I began to fill the reservoir of my mind with forward-looking thoughts. What interesting people would I meet? Would there be new foods to taste? How could this experience affect my life?

The time away was filled with the exhilara-tion of seeing beautiful, inspirational gardens as well as other joys I hadn't anticipated. So, by unplugging the negative and being flexible, it became possible for positive energy to flow freely.

You, too, can have this joyful play be part of your life when you face a task that you would rather not do. All you need to do is ask the question, "How can I change the hard tasks into pleasurable experiences?" To change your mind-set, literally turn your body in the opposite direction as you ask this question. You can write down your new plan so that it becomes imprinted in your mind. Leave spaces in your plan for unexpected "Aha!" experiences that you might discover along the way.

I think that as we face the challenges in life and move forward, this continuous flow of harmony can lead us to a healthy, happy path as we honor all parts of our bodies working together in unity.

Work and play then become an exciting balancing act!

EMMA SCHULER

For as long as I can remember, Emma lived on Main Street in our town. For the last few years she lived, I became fascinated watching this elderly lady as she took care of her garden, chopped ice, and shoveled snow. I often thought about all the wonderful stories she might have about her life in this small town. Of one thing I was sure: She must have had a lot of secrets for a long and healthy life. I wanted to talk with her, as she always seemed so alone, but instead, I only watched her from across the street. She lived to be in her nineties and to this day she lives on in my mind. She taught me silently.

Her way of working was to do a little raking, a little weeding, a little planting almost as if she purposely had a special rhythm. I wondered why she did that, but looking back now, I think perhaps her garden was her song of life.

Like most young people, I was impatient to finish tasks quickly. My mother's message was very clear: Finish one job before you go on to another so that you can cross it off the list. Consequently, when I did my gardening, I thought the way to do it was to do *all* the weeding, then *all* the digging, *all* the planting, and then *all* the watering, in that order. I'd end up exhausted and with a terrible headache. Through the years, the picture of Emma would keep coming back. She lived in my memory as a beautiful teacher.

Today when I work in the garden, I think of her and how she changed my life. I play beautiful music or simply listen to the music of nature. My energy keeps replenishing, and I almost always finish refreshed and filled with peace. This is what she must have felt! She lived in harmony with her land.

As I walk over the farm today, I am reminded of my old self as the workers plod on to complete only one task at a time instead of rotating jobs to make the work more interesting and less straining. Why do so many of us feel that we must end one job before going on to the next?

How can we inspire each other to harmoniously blend work together by sometimes doing multiple tasks, a bit at a time, so that our energy and interest last longer? This is a lesson that we can carry into every aspect of our lives, at work and with our families. And yes, we can blend work and leisure together. It's that rhythm that refreshes. Perhaps we need more people like Emma to gently touch our minds so that we may be more deeply inspired to live in harmony with our gardens, our earth, our souls, and each other.

TAKE CARE OF YOU

I heard a commentator ask the question, "Where will you be in 20 years? How can you make your dreams and goals happen?"

We need to stir up that creative imagination and expand horizons; having a positive outlook helps us stay healthy.

Sometimes we are faced with challenges that we have not anticipated. They are the peaks and valleys that mark the road map of life, and they come in all shapes and sizes, at all times, and in all places. When we are faced with these experiences, we need to ask ourselves sooner, "What am I going to do about it? How can I learn and grow from this experience?"

Remember that happiness, peace, and love are not "in" things somewhere "out" there. They are found inside us, and, like planting a garden, they need to be nurtured in order to flower. Here is my prescription for health.

• It's *okay* to be who you are. You only need to be in competition with yourself to make a better you!

• Forgive yourself for not being perfect.

• Say no to risky behavior.

• Treat yourself the way you would treat your best friend.

• Throw away the resentment you might have for other people.

• Don't emphasize problems that cause pain.

• Realize how much your family loves you.

• Reach out to help others and give encouragement, but at the same time, make sure that your needs are tenderly cared for.

• When it comes to your well-being, maintain your independence.

• Keep optimistic and honest.

• Houseclean your mind and get rid of baggage not needed anymore.

• Rethink organizations and groups you belong to and shed those that are outgrown.

• Eat nourishing meals even if you are alone and add music and candlelight.

• Eat less meat and more fresh vegetables—take your vitamins!

• Exercise daily.

• Make a morning thankful list for all the beauty that surrounds you.

• Make an evening thankful list for all those people who were special throughout the day.

I urge you to take walks and let the beauty of life touch your spirit. Hold the earth and its people close to your heart. The quest for health, harmony, and happiness is endless and elegantly wonderful. Your life can make a positive difference for a better world. Remember always—it begins with you!

CHAPTER 2

Compassion

We are each of us angels with only one wing,
and we can fly only by embracing each other.

LUCIANO DE CRESCENZO

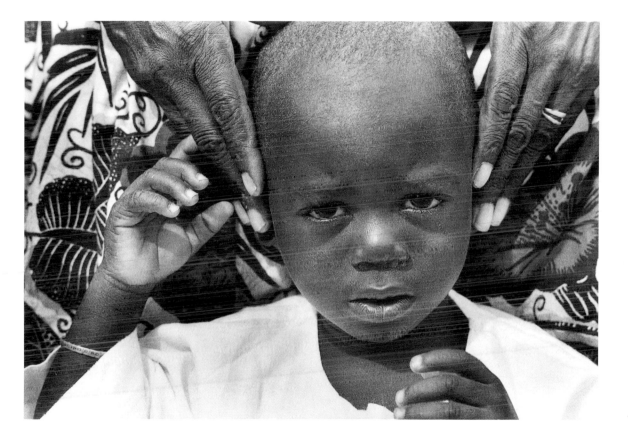

DOGS HAVE
SOULS, TOO

My late husband, Bob, was so relieved that our home had become dog-free at last. With four lively children and a house always filled with visitors, it was one less hassle to deal with.

Two of my older children and a niece who spent a lot of time with us decided to go to an animal auction. Bob gave them strict instructions to come home empty-handed. Of course, they couldn't resist purchasing a little brown and black ball of fur for $1.87, including tax. There was trouble ahead!

We decided to put the puppy, whom we named Kiki, in one of the buildings on the farm, with a clock wrapped in a towel. All would be safe, we thought, but its pitiful cries traveled through our open windows, and Bob was angry. They would have to take it back the next day, he insisted. Of course, the animal auction was closed the next day, and Kiki began to win all our hearts, even Bob's.

Because we lived on a farm, she had com-plete freedom to follow the children around. I don't ever remember her being on a leash—just being close to us was tie enough for her. As Kiki grew, she branched out in her social circle, greeting visitors with her great doggie smile and waving-fan tail. She even wandered to the nearby country club in summertime to greet each person who sat around the pool. After receiving her positive strokes, she would return home. She was filled with love—receiving and giving.

There were periods of my life when I was sad or felt overworked, and I would retreat to a quiet corner on the farm, sit on the grass, and talk to myself about how wonderful it would be to be cheered. Only Kiki, with her "sixth sense," would find me and gently lay her head on my lap. I often asked her, "Kiki, when you're sad, where do you go when you need love? I appreciate you, who so freely give of your love and compassion. I love you."

In her twelfth year, Kiki developed arthritis and found it hard to get around. Each night, I would play beautiful music on the stereo in the living room, and she would immediately hobble as close to the speakers as she could. With her eyes half closed, she listened as if she were part of the symphony. Was she reliving her past, or just being present in the moment? Was she trying to make each of those moments in her life treasured ones? She was so much a part of the family that I doubt whether she made any distinction between herself and us.

The sad day came when she left us. During her life she had taught us about loyalty, compassion, and love. How lucky we were to have her share her life with us!

GIFTS OF HEART AND HANDS

In summer through my growing years, Mother always kept our hands busy. We stayed out of trouble as we busily made all the gifts for our family and many relatives for the holidays. I continued this creative joy until after I was married, and then times changed. It appeared that handmade gifts weren't perceived as good enough anymore. I stopped this tradition except for two special friends who continued to make their gifts for me.

The word *gift* in the dictionary is defined as "something voluntarily transferred from one person to another without compensation; talent."

At a recent conference I attended, as part of the program we were asked to give away one of our possessions. We were not told beforehand that this would be asked of us. There was little chance to prepare ourselves for this ceremony. I had packed for this trip with the bare minimum, and I labored over what my gift might be. The only thing I had to give away was my rainbow scarf that I dearly loved. As you know, it is easy to give away things you don't want anymore, but to release a possession that is special is very hard. We entered the large ballroom in silence as each one of the 500 people came with their gifts. With a tear in my eye, I gently laid my scarf in the center circle.

"Good-bye, dear friend," I said. I watched very closely to see who might pick my gift, and when I saw the happiness on the face of the woman who received it, I knew it was in warm hands. A feeling of release swept over me.

As I write this, I realize that my most precious "Giveaway" was the panel for the AIDS quilt, which I lovingly made for my son, David, who died from AIDS in December of 1985. He was just 30 years old. As I stitched away, there were so many wonderful memories of happy times we shared together. The quilt had become part of me. I gave it away as so many other parents and friends have done to serve as a reminder to the world of the need for education and to help others realize the impact of taking care—to live and to share unconditional love!

When you approach any season of gift giving, please remember the words of poet Robert Lowell when he wrote in *The Vision of Sir Launfal*:

Not what we give, but what we share,
The gift without the giver is bare:
Who gives himself with his alms feeds three,
Himself, his hungering neighbor, and me.

SWIMMING UPSTREAM

I have a recurring dream: I'm swimming for all my worth against the tide. No matter how hard I try, little progress is made. Exhaustion sets in, and I wonder if I will survive. Then, very gently, I feel a hand on my shoulder. It seems as if someone is there to help me onward. My fight to stay afloat eases, and all of a sudden there is the assurance that I am not alone. The fear subsides, and I begin to relax.

Several of us at work were discussing this one morning, and I asked if anyone had ever had a similar feeling. One man said that he had the experience of an imaginary hand touching him when he was bike riding in a race. Another person chimed in that this happened to him when he was near the finish line in a running race as the last hill loomed before him.

And then, I remembered my mother's

favorite picture. It was one of a little girl with her arm around her small brother as they crossed a treacherous bridge in the midst of a very dark storm. Behind them was the most beautiful guardian angel stretching her arms over them with care. That picture was a reminder to us children that there was a loving, helping hand hovering over us as we faced hard experiences in life.

Sometimes that hand is real. A number of years ago I was in the emergency room at the hospital in excruciating pain. A complicated spinal tap was being performed, and all of a sudden a doctor's hand reached out to hold mine. I'll never forget that feeling of comfort.

Have you had experiences in your life when it seemed as if you were fighting life's elements, and suddenly you were touched by a helping hand? That hand, real or imaginary, seems to quiet the mind and give us that extra feeling of confidence that we will accomplish our goals or be safe from harm. It could be a hand of protection, a hand of friendship, or a hand of love that touches our lives.

As we have guardian angels helping us, so we, too, can be guardian angels for someone else who needs care in the midst of concern.

Hold a child who is hurt. Touch someone with cancer or AIDS to let him know that you are there for support. Touch a friend or a pet. Reach out to the aged and those who are alone.

In my growing up, I had lots of old aunts and uncles who treated me with dignity, but in all our visits we didn't touch. Aunt Elizabeth went to a nursing home, and, like her aging friends, she had few visitors. The last time I visited her she looked so sad. My hands cradled her face, and as I looked into her eyes and kissed her I told her, "I love you." The tears trickled down her worn face. How many years had passed since someone had spoken those words to her?

Please look at your hands with palms upward. Be a receiver of the healing angel touch. And then, as you turn your hand over, reach out to others to be their special angel.

REACHING OUT

As we travel through life, we all experience valleys that grab us with fear, pain or sadness, and we wonder how we will survive. Looking at my early life, I know that our family held a lot of love for each other, but we went through life not touching each other in times of trial.

I was in my early twenties when my father had his fourth heart attack. It happened when Mother and Father were at the summer cabin. Mother didn't drive, so she waited a couple of days before she walked to the village to call the doctor. The doctor called Daddy's two sisters, my cousin, and me to tell us that we needed to go to him because this would be the last time we would see him alive. We went that afternoon and found Daddy on the couch by the fireplace. Tears rolled down his face as he sobbed, but all of us stood at the door and watched him. For the first time, I saw the hurt little boy in a man's body, and I felt his aloneness; yet not one of us went to console him and tell him he had made a difference in our lives. Even though we grow up to think of our-

selves as islands, we do have the ability to change because someone has touched our lives in a meaningful way.

It never occurred to me that it would be helpful for someone to go with me for the doctor's verdict on a pending operation, but a young friend insisted on accompanying me, and I was tremendously comforted by her presence. As the time approached for the operation, my whole family was busy, each with his own agenda, and I felt so isolated and sad. So I decided to write my family a letter telling them that I had always been there for them and that now I was asking them to be with me. To my surprise, they all dropped their plans and each one took turns helping me. Perhaps their busyness was a cover-up for being as scared as I was.

My niece, Dana, is a nurse, and she told me that she would be with me for the operation. As we entered the operating room, she introduced me to each specially chosen doctor and nurse. As each one was introduced, they held my hand or cradled me in their arms. "I had the same operation that you will have and

I am fine," one said, while another told me, "I took care of your son when he was in the hospital. He was such a grand person." Then, as I was ready to go under anesthesia, Dana led me on a meditation walk. She asked me to think of a place where I felt at peace, and I smiled as I thought of my beautiful garden. Next, she asked what I saw there and my reply was, "The faces of all those people I love." I went to sleep then, and when I awoke, my daughter was there to tell me I had cancer.

After these experiences, I would never be the same. Being able to feel love became a strong lifeline for crossing the bridge to touch others who need care. We can all be vehicles of compassion by lending our hands, our arms, and our hearts. All it takes is that softening touch of someone close by to ease the fear, the sadness, and the pain, and to say, "I am here" as a family, friend, or stranger.

Reach out to touch others and feel the healing begin!

CAR ACCIDENT

I was home alone and had just gone to bed. The front doorbell rang frantically. A man called to me, "There's been a bad accident in front of your house. Call the police!"

I did and then dressed hurriedly and rushed out to the highway to see a car flipped on its hood. Glass lay all over the highway and I cried, "Holy cow! I don't see how anyone could get out of this alive!"

A young blond-headed boy stood by the side of the road. Shivering profusely, he looked at me and replied, "I was in that car."

I was aware that he was in shock, so I took him close to me and wrapped him in the folds of my cape. Finally I said, "You need a blanket. I'll go get you one." He told me that there was a blanket in his car. Peeping out from under, I saw it amid the glass. I crawled under and pulled it out and shook out the glass shards.

As I fastened it tightly around him, he looked in my eyes and said, "Where do you live? You must be somebody's mother!" I said, "I live right here, and yes, I'm doing for you what I hope someone would do for my son if he were in your shoes."

I thought about him often and wondered what might have happened to him. Many years passed.

Just recently I was at a reception near my home, and a young man, his blond hair in a ponytail, came and stood before me. He looked vaguely familiar as he smiled and said, "I guess you don't remember me. I was in an accident in front of your home a long time ago. You cared for me. Through the years I wanted to see you, and I never had the opportunity until tonight."

I felt the tears in my eyes, and I saw the mist in his as we hugged. I still don't know his name.

LOSING SOMEONE CLOSE

Dear Lee,
I have asked myself so many times over these past few years, "How do you get over the pain of losing someone you love?" I think it happens like planting a garden and watching it grow—a little bit at a time.

I'd like to share some of the things I am doing that have helped me ease my sadness. On the month anniversary of the loss, I buy myself a beautiful rose, or pick one from the garden in summer and display it in a prominent place. The rose is a reminder to the whole family of our loved one.

On the birthdays of each of my children, I do something special just for me. It might be a pleasant walk or buying more beautiful flowers, but it is always a quiet respite where I have time to reflect on how much they mean to me —or meant to me.

Special remembering days should be a celebration where the community of those who love and care come together. The first birthday that my son David was gone, I decided to have a party. I invited 11 of his closest friends to come to dinner. They were all excited and without my telling them, they remembered that special date. I brought the big dining room table into the living room and placed it in front of the warm fireplace. I had prepared all of David's favorite foods, and we all sat around sharing great David stories. Our spirits were uplifted.

Treat yourself with love, care for yourself, surround yourself with beauty, give yourself love pats and dwell on the positive. If you have any regrets, forgive yourself; we are all human and God forgives all. So should we, even ourselves. Instead of running, give yourself quiet walks, time to discover nature, time to sit in the sun or a sunlit window and capture the rainbows. Take time to contemplate in our wonderful world and surround yourself with caring people.

At work I often encounter people who are ill or in the process of a divorce, and they are grieving, too. So I think this message of getting over the pain of loss is meant for them as well.

Regeneration from suffering is a lonely path, but good can come from it. It can lead you into yourself to touch your spirit so that a warm fire glows inside your heart. That fire is kindled to purify the sadness and turn it into joy once more. Only then, as we share with others, do we heal and realize that helping others, along the path of life's journey gives us strength and peace.

One day, after my son and husband were no longer here, I saw a wonderful, cuddly stuffed monkey in a store. I couldn't resist buying it, and now, every night when I go to sleep, the soft little animal is in my arms and it gives me comfort as I go to sleep.

The flowers and this teddy bear are for you —to help you heal.

Peace and love,
Ardie

YOU CAN FACE THE SUN

Do any of you remember the World War II song "Pack Up Your Troubles In Your Old Kitbag and Smile, Smile, Smile"? It was an extremely popular song. It presented a strong message that people needed to hear at that time. We, too, need to hear the same kind of optimistic message when we are facing the battle against stress.

A short time ago, I wrote in my diary: "Sometimes I feel as though there's a giant winch pulling me tighter and tighter as I pack much more into my days than I should. If only all this stress in my life would disappear."

Do you feel like this at times? Today this feeling is spreading at an amazing rate to children as well as adults. Stress alters our balance. To be healthy, we need to discover ways to bring that balance back. I have a few suggestions for you.

First of all, there are some situations for which there just don't seem to be any solutions no matter how hard we try to find them. We tend to focus on the predicament so exclusively that a deep forest from which we can't find our way out seems to surround us. But there are things we can do that help.

• Visualize a box that you can put all your stress in. Then imagine digging a deep hole and burying your box of stress in it. As you pile earth on top of it, breathe deeply. Say to yourself, "I don't need to carry that box with me any longer." Feel good about all that weight that your mind has released. Amazingly, after you've done this, the answer to your problem comes to you like the dawning of a new day.

• Keep a stack of imaginary envelopes by your bed. Before you go to sleep, slip each stressful thought into a mental envelope, seal it, and drop it in the mailbox. Destination: out of mind, no return address!

• Picture a small, weightless feather in the palm of your hand. Think of the feather as your problems and pretend to blow them to the wind. Watch them as they are wafted away to land on new territory.

• Clear your mind before going to bed. My late husband, Bob, used to keep a pencil and paper by the bed so he could jot down what he needed to remember for the next day. By doing this he was able to relieve his mind and rest peacefully.

• When stress takes over at work, clear your head by changing the scenery. Go outside instead of taking a coffee break. Let nature touch your heart and mind. Touch the earth. Hug a tree. Take deep breaths. Say to yourself, "Thank you. I am alive and well."

• Meditate for 20 minutes each day. It can be as rejuvenating as an hour's nap.

• Take a warm bath by candlelight while you listen to soft music. Hug yourself and know that you are a special person, one who has a lot to contribute to a healthy world.

• Reach out to your loved ones. I think back to when my children were small and their energy was unbounded even though they were tired. They were on a merry-go-round that wouldn't stop. I held them lovingly, and as I rocked and hummed to them, their frenzy gradually changed to peace.

• Remember how soothing it was to be held by someone close when you were small? We are no different today. When my son died from AIDS, I would often say to my husband, "Hold me. Soothe away this stressful pain." We can do that for each other now—children, family, friends. Reach out to touch one another with tenderness, and feel that warm quilt of relaxation surround you with love. Perhaps this is the most powerful stress reducer of all.

When my children were small, they learned a song in nursery school with these words: "When you are in trouble, the devil wears a grin, so open up your heart and let the sun shine in." It's so simple. Answers come to us when we face the sun. You can do that!

Grief

Some people think it's holding on
that makes one strong; sometimes it's letting go.

S Y L V I A   R O B I N S O N

GIFTS
OF THE SPIRIT

We have come almost a full circle for another year. Many people are rushing toward the holidays to finish all the last-minute details. Where are we rushing to? Pause a while in silence to think about counting the many blessings that have come your way.

I'd like to share with you a tender part of my life. After my son David and my husband, Bob, died, there were periods of extreme sadness, and I wondered how I would survive. Holiday times, as you may have experienced, are particularly hard. Sometimes, in the midst of all the merriment, you might feel very alone.

At such times, it has helped me to know that energy never dies. It just takes on another dimension. Often, after they were no longer here, I wondered how I could cope, and I cried out, "Let me know that you are with me! What do I do?" I never got the "What do I do?" message, but I have gotten the "I am here with you" message.

That message comes in the form of feathers. One day in my anguish, as I walked the fields, I looked down and there at my feet was a beautiful white feather. With tears in my eyes, I gently picked it up to carry home. Another day, when I unlocked the door, there were two perfectly formed white feathers right there on the stoop. I find feathers now wherever I go even though I don't look for them. I have begun to feel each time as if it is an "Aha!" experience, and I am not alone. I feel that Bob and David are continually with me from up in the heavens and seeing me grow stronger every day. Could they be heavenly cheerleaders?

Perhaps you have seen the movie *Forrest Gump*. His wife died. The movie started out with feathers wafting in the atmosphere. He, too, had the feeling that his wife was with him when his eyes saw unexpected feathers as he faced important times in life and needed a gentle touch.

Much of my philosophy comes from the

Native Americans, who believe that all life is sacred. To them, feathers are gifts of the spirit and can give us strength and courage.

Native Americans have a special ceremony called potlatch, or the Give Away ceremony. They give away *not* things they don't want anymore but things that are important in their lives. The lesson to be learned is that we should not become overly attached to material things because it is only the spirit that is eternal. There can be an exhilarating feeling of release as we are able to give these things away.

Even though I have only read about this ceremony, it has deeply affected me, as I believe that my feathers were given to me as a spiritual gift. Just lately, I have added the dimension of the Give Away ceremony to my life. I give these treasured feathers to other people who need care, hoping that they, too, might be lifted up in spirit as I have become. I feel filled with joy!

I'm sure that each one of you, in your own way, have experienced gifts of the spirit. Perhaps your list might include warm hugs, a flower, a meal, a beautiful stone that reflects light, or a prism that causes rainbows to dance in the sunlight.

How can you share your gifts with those who need to be lifted up on eagle wings? These gifts, most of them from nature or from the well of your heart, are there for all of us to give. It can help you, as it has helped me, to be filled with peace and understanding and light. Ah, how precious life is! Please *do* share your gifts of the spirit.

OVERCOMING GRIEF — A TRUE STORY

I felt like a young child again. The day was bright and shiny—the last warm day of fall. With springy steps, I took a walk over the farm. I was so glad to be alive. It was David's thirtieth birthday. Later he came to my office, and I asked him how it felt to be 30. He replied, "Gee, Mom, I don't feel any different." With a smile I answered, "Well, I can tell you one thing. Life gets better. I am so much happier now than when I was 30." That night after dinner, he started to hyperventilate.

What could be wrong with David? As I looked at him in the next few days, a feeling of uneasiness began to creep into my mind and fear gripped my soul. In less than two weeks he died from pneumocystis due to AIDS. He was diagnosed just two days before his death. I wasn't there when his time came. As I entered the hospital room immediately afterward, he looked so peaceful. My first reaction was not one of grief. Instead, I felt overwhelming love for this wonderful son who I was so proud of. I thought about bringing him into the world, and I felt the urgency to somehow return him to my body. As I rubbed my hand over his still warm, strong arm, I prayed, "Thanks, God, for the privilege to be David's Mom. If only I could have had him with me a while longer." I realized that my terrible fear of death was all gone, and then the feeling of loss surrounded me like a tightening band.

The day after the service celebrating his life, there was a new snowfall. I walked the same path over the farm as I did the day of his birthday. The tears never stopped and the wind was pushing me from behind. As I got to the end of the field and turned around to come home, my tears stopped and the wind was now pushing me from the front. I heard a voice inside of me saying, "First I'll help you—and then you need to help yourself." I looked down at the new footprints in the snow and realized that my life was creating a new uncharted path. How could I manage without David? It was as if a part of me was missing.

The anguish didn't stop. I feel that the hardest experience in life is the death of a child. The parent thinks of all the unfulfilled dreams that will never come to pass, and the sorrow goes deep within the heart.

Healing from grief takes a long time. It begins with one step at a time. When I went back to work, I found it difficult to concentrate and often, in meetings, my mind would wander. It was hard to make decisions. When people would ask how I was doing, I'd reply, "Fine," and then there was a rush of tears. I asked myself, "Would other people understand and have patience with me?" One woman asked me to play an active part in a college meeting, and I told her I couldn't because my grief was still too strong. She said to me, "You hold up well. To look at you no one would ever know." How could she be so insensitive! I was angry, and then I realized that she had never experienced the death of a child, and in my heart I forgave her.

One day in the midst of my tears, the doorbell rang and there were two little neighbor boys there. They asked if they could come in. We got out my grandchildren's toys. As they were filled with wonder and excitement, sunshine came to my face. The power of children's laughter can be a healing balm.

David was an ardent collector of papers and things. Since his house was small, much of what he didn't immediately need was stored at our home. I asked my husband, Bob, what I would ever do with all the things. I felt exhausted. He said, "Just put it in a closet." When I finally did get around to putting his things in order, all the memories came flooding back, and I was devastated. The biggest lesson I learned was never to clean out during or right after any special occasion, anniversary, or holiday. Grief at this time is a double whammy!

I realized more than ever that we are not islands in our lives. We are surrounded by many friends who love and care for us. They are there to share happiness or be sad with us. This was shown very clearly by the number of cards and letters that came in stacks delivered by the mailman. One day, I sat at the kitchen table and sighed. I thought to myself, "I am breathing in all this love and health, and as I exhale, out go all negative thoughts and disease." I was always a good giver but never a good receiver, and this was a time to learn. We are all there for each other to be an arm of support and love. As my son Anthony said, "We are all grieving, but Mom, remember that the rest of us are still here."

As I was David's cheerleader in his life, his spiritual urging now became mine. I felt him encouraging me on to reach out to other people—to help them understand about AIDS. In a sense, his life was being carried on through me. My unconditional love for him helped open my heart. I like to think of healing from grief as the beginning of a tight bud—gradually, the petals unfold and with time reach out to be a beautiful flower.

Four years after David left, my mother was dying. I had been reading a lot about how to say good-bye to someone you love. While her mind was still clear, I figured the time had come for me to tell her how much she meant to me. She listened for a while and then had a look of indignation on her face. She said to me, "Don't tell me when I am ready; I'll tell you." I laughed and said, "Okay, Mother." If I wouldn't have told her that day, it would have been too late. Another stroke left her incoherent. Her process took three months, and there were many days that we thought would be her last. I was with her when she died, stroking her forehead and saying over and over, "I love you, Mother."

I thought the circle of Mother's life was closed and that I had done all my grieving before she died. I went back to work immediately and had one accident after another. What I had to learn was that grieving doesn't end abruptly. While one life might be over, we need to treat ourselves with tender care. We are not machines at a time like this, but special, fragile human beings.

I believe that tragedy happens in threes. My husband, Bob, and I were both so busy. Our work was unified, even though it took us in different directions. I came home from one trip just as Bob was ready to go on another.

This time, he was going to Russia to culminate a joint venture between Rodale Press and that country on agriculture. On the day he was due to arrive home, I thought that it would be so wonderful to settle down together for a while. I was filled with excitement as I anticipated his homecoming. I wore a new red skirt. At noon, two of my daughters and one of the presidents of the company appeared at my office door and blurted out that Bob had been killed on the way to the airport to come home. I screamed, "No, no! Take it all away!" My mind held utter disbelief! It couldn't be true, but yes, it was. We got through all the plans and decided to have his service on the farm that he loved so much. Two thousand people attended his life celebration. When we came back from the cemetery, there were people walking and picnicking all over the farm and I thought, "Wow, Bob would really love this!"

The days went by, and I felt as if I was in a fog. I still felt that Bob was away on a trip and would soon be home. I began to wonder why I didn't seem to have any feeling. Where was reality? I mentioned this to my son Anthony, and he told me that I needed to see a counselor. He said that if he weren't having counseling when Bob died, he never would have made it. The counselor told me that I had too much sadness in a short period of time, and that this was nature's way of allowing me only what I could handle at the time. She said that feeling would come back. It did, but not until I felt rebellion and probably suppressed anger at Bob: "How could you leave me?"

I have learned that we do have a choice on how we will deal with grief. If it is bottled up inside of us, we can become ill. We need to gradually let it go. It is not an easy flow because it comes back in waves. With time we can be filled with calmness. I have worked hard at finding peace. When adversity comes, we need to rest a while, contemplate, and allow quiet time for gaining strength. True understanding comes about as we allow it to become part of us, and realize that we can see that good can come through adversity.

I like to think of the story of the oyster. A tiny grain of sand can work its way into the shell and cause pain for the oyster, but the pain doesn't destroy it—instead, over time, the oyster produces a beautiful pearl.

In the play *Zorba the Greek,* someone asks Zorba what he does when he is sad. His reply is, "I dance." For me, I have learned to go out to do something for someone else who needs cheer and love.

Sometimes now, I look at myself as a tree that has withstood many storms.

I have bent with the stress of it all but have always snapped back taller and stronger than before.

I would never trade my life for another. The special people in my life will always be warm in my heart and, if I am quiet, I hear them urging me to keep on helping others to make a difference. Energy never dies. It becomes a star burst when it changes direction, and it glows with a brighter light of understanding when it comes down to touch us all who are still here to carry on. I am thankful for life and each new day.

F O G

How often have you heard someone say, "Oh, they are in a fog." Thinking about that, it probably means that they don't know where they are going.

I thought about that the other morning when very early I opened the side door to step out for my walk. The daylight should have been appearing, but the fog was so heavy, I could not see farther than five feet in front of me. There were only my feet to guide me over the path as I looked down. I said to myself, "Don't panic and fight the fog. Let it envelop you." I had faith that I would find my way. I was ready for surprise. I stopped in my tracks and breathed in the absolute silence as a rare gift. I was filled with a sense of great mystery as I stepped out into space. I asked, "What else would I encounter that wasn't there yesterday?"

As I walked along in the sea of nothingness, my mind went back to the old Sherlock Holmes mystery movies where a sinister figure walked in the dense fog and appeared under a dimly lit streetlight trying to find his way.

Then my thoughts were diverted by the wail of a train whistle in the faraway distance. I thought back in time when I was in college and went to Europe. The ship I took was a converted troop ship, and for two days the dense fog made it impossible to see what might be out there. This experience happened before radar. So every five minutes, the foghorn blew to let other ships know, "I am here." Occasionally, another foghorn would answer back. It was comforting to me to know that on this great sea of space, we were not alone.

I thought about a blind man I had seen several days before, walking along the street tapping his cane. He was feeling his way and appeared to be confident in his ability, showing no fear. He had learned to rely on his other senses. He walked with utter trust. I realized that this was what I was doing in that walk in the fog.

Fog surrounds us not only in nature, but through our experiences in life. It could be the result of an illness, loss of a loved one, losing a job, the dilemma of moving on to a new position, overwork, or an unsolved problem. The list is endless. Do you feel afraid at a time like this?

To find solutions, sometimes it becomes necessary to go through the fog and look inward. Instead of rebelling, we can use this quiet time to help us sort out and clarify our thinking. It's like going through a valley.

Then, as the fog begins to lift, our eyes shift from looking downward to being lifted up toward the horizon. Our senses join and expand to be fully aware of the larger world and the people in it who care for and mother us. Through this experience we gain the strength to move forward. We don't need to stay lost. The fog has become a cloak of love, till we are ready to have the confidence to step out once again on the stage of life.

CHAPTER 4

Happiness

Sing, shout, celebrate the happiness of life.

UNKNOWN

MAGIC KINGDOM

When you think of the Magic Kingdom, what comes to mind? Do you think of Disney World, where imagination comes to life with joy and wonder? Do you think of being a child again and expanding your mind in new directions?

To some people the Magic Kingdom might be in other people, in going on a vacation, or in their work. Still others might feel that their Magic Kingdom could be within their families or their homes or what happens in leisure time. I imagine that there would be tremendous variation in everyone's responses.

Each year, I am invited to a party at a friend's house, and I see an unbelievable sight. He uses a very large part of his basement for creating a cyclorama of intricately moving figures. The German word for this is *putz*. Each year he expands the amazing design. There are at least 14 trains going through mountain passes. Skiers actually ski down snowy slopes and skaters twirl over the ice. The Ferris wheel is all decked out in rainbow lights. If my friend were asked, his Magic Kingdom might be his creative ingenuity to build this spectacular vision of Utopia. He is so thrilled to see his masterpiece through the eyes of his grandchildren and many friends.

As I close my eyes to think of this, my mind is filled with whirling visions as I, too, continually create my Magic Kingdom. To me it is a place that feels safe with a warm, fuzzy feeling of love. There is comfort, joy, peace and contentment, candlelight, soft music, high energy, and family surrounding me. There are many special friends, smiling children's faces and remembrances of good times. Delicious aromas of nostalgic foods fill the air, and there is a reaching out of hope for a world filled with unity, love, and peace. I know my Magic Kingdom is tucked in my heart. I want to continally build and enhance this dream because it is all that has made me who I am today. I am grateful!

I hope that you, too, will exercise your imagination, build your dreams, and plan what your Magic Kingdom means to you. As you hold it close, may it hold wonder beyond your wildest dreams!

HAPPINESS
IS AN ECSTASY

Happiness is an ecstasy that we all strive for, and yet it so often eludes us because our minds and bodies are racing ahead to tomorrow instead of enjoying today.

Perhaps our lives are encumbered with too much activity and possessions so that we feel we have to get rid of the cobwebs hindering our vision before we can see the sun of happiness. People spend so much time making the journey *to* happiness that they fail to realize it is the journey itself that *is* happiness. The frustration of working so hard to achieve happiness can be a major reason for stress taking over our lives.

If this happens to you, remember the words at the railroad crossing. *Stop! Look! Listen!*

Stop when your life is encumbered with stress. Breathe deeply to oxygenate every cell in your body.

Look to change your view and find what stands in the way of happiness.

Listen to the message that suggests that maybe you are looking in the wrong place.

Perhaps our adult world has made us forget the joys of spontaneity that we felt as young children. How long has it been since you sat in the outdoors and painted pictures in cloud formations, listened to the singing of the birds, or shuffled your feet through a pile of autumn leaves? What about marveling at a beautiful sunrise or a sunset?

All of us travel many paths in life searching for happiness. Most often we are searching for it outside of ourselves. One of my grandchildren opened my eyes to a new depth of understanding of happiness. One evening, she said to me, "Ummy, build a house." We got out the blocks. Going through my mind were bricks, wood, and furnishings; her small 2^1/$_2$-year-old mind had a different agenda. Smiling all the while as she placed each block in position, she named a family member and those people close to her. For her a house was not built of material things but was a structure of people, perhaps ideas and dreams.

Allow yourself the freedom of living in the

present moment. Realize that the center of happiness comes from inside you and nourishes how you feel about yourself. See and appreciate all the beauty and kindness that come to you and what you can give to others. There appears the soft touch of the beat of life radiat-ing from within. You *can* find it in the center of who you are. Here reside peace, fulfilling energy and, ultimately, happiness. The gift you give yourself is very precious. You can carry it with you wherever you go. May the light of happiness surround you!

BLUEBIRDS

I have a friend who lives in a place called Bluebird Meadows. I have never been there, and I continually wonder what kind of magical place it must be. I imagine bluebirds living in a paradise—a meadow filled with the most beautiful colored flowers that gently sway in the breeze.

It reminds me of the wonderful children's story called "The Blue Bird" by Maurice Maeterlinck. It is the story of two children who had incredible faith that if they searched hard enough, they would find the Bluebird of Happiness. They were told that if the bluebird could be found, they would have knowledge of everything. They asked themselves, "Must we know everything to be happy?" Excited, they set out on their journey. The advice they received before leaving was, "Seek! Don't be afraid of experience or what you might discover."

The first place the children searched was in memories past, but happiness was not there. Next, they searched into the future, but the bluebird and the happiness they sought were not there either.

Finally, after a long journey, the bluebird appeared, and you can imagine the children's joy. Then, the specter of fear entered their hearts, and they felt that in order to keep the bird safe, they should put it in a cage. The poor bluebird became a prisoner, his heart grew sad, and he hung his head and died.

How often do we hold on with a tight fist to those we love because of fear? They, too, can feel as if they are in a cage. The children in the story learned a valuable lesson early in their lives: As painful as it might be to open up their fists and let go of possessions, it was the only way for happiness to live. They discovered that in the giving and sharing of themselves, happiness is found in love.

I think back to high school days, when one local radio station played the same song three times at regular intervals throughout the long night. Sometimes, I would try to stay up all night to hear Jan Pierce sing "The Bluebird of Happiness." It was a song full of hope. The words went something like this: "Hold your head up high, you'll find greater peace of mind when you listen to the song. Remember the world is full of bliss. Somewhere there's a bluebird of happiness."

We can give momentary happiness to others, but lasting happiness occurs when joy finds a home within our hearts, and we give ourselves the freedom to be who we are.

THE GIFT OF JOY

I took a trip to the island of Maui not too long ago; it was a respite that I eagerly anticipated because it would offer me some real contemplation time. Early each morning, I would walk along the ocean path.

Wow! One morning, I looked across the bay and there, hovering over the far-off town, was a huge, fat, vibrant rainbow!

At home the rainbows usually are pale and disappear very rapidly. I wondered how long this amazing arc of many colors would last and kept my eyes constantly on the heavens.

As I walked, I came up behind a mother and her daughter. I listened briefly to their conversation and noticed that all the while they were speaking, the mother never raised her head. Finally, I couldn't contain my thoughts any longer. I said, "Do you see that glorious rainbow?"

The mother looked up and replied, "I never even noticed. Thank you."

The daughter answered in a matter-of-fact way, "I saw one yesterday on the walk."

I thought about this and wondered if we share enough joy in our lives.

Michele, my secretary, had a face filled with sunshine as she told me about her drive home one evening. As the rain ended, a huge arc of a rainbow filled the sky. She shared her surprise with me, and vicariously, I enjoyed the magic of what she saw. We all need to share the glories that we experience each day. All too often we lock it up inside of us. It becomes double joy when it is shared.

You need not wait for one of those rare occasions to see a rainbow after the storm. *You* can touch a rainbow in your home or place of work! Hang a prism in a window where the sun shines through. At unexpected times, rainbows will dance around your room. This can become an "Aha!" experience that can fill you with joy.

Our lives are like the prism. There are many facets that make up our total being. We realize that we need both sunshine and sorrow, tears and laughter, to make us appreciate our days. We grow by the way the pendulum swings between the two extremes. It depends on how we look at life to realize the depth of what we see. We might see only the tears, but if we are optimistic, we look through the tears to see the hope that lies beyond. That's when the rainbow reflects life's glory.

I send prisms to friends who are grieving. This message accompanies my gift:

"Please hang this prism in a window where the sun shines through. At unexpected times you will see rainbows dancing. Let this be a happy reminder that even though the one you love is not physically here, his energy never dies and his spirit is alive and well, dancing in the hearts of all those who love that person still."

RAINBOWS

It's so wonderfully mind-expanding to be among children. I was asked to read a story to a kindergarten and first grade class, and the book I chose was all about rainbows. We not only see them in the sky, but we can find them in many unexpected places. To all of us, rainbows bring hope and happiness.

The story was about Lori, who saw a huge arc of rainbow in the sky. Both ends of the rainbow seemed to touch the earth. It disappeared before she was finished looking at its glory, and she felt sad. She decided that she could paint a picture of a rainbow so that she would always have it close to her. When she was finished, she announced that she was going outside to look for other rainbows, but her mother told her she would have to wait for more rain. Her reply was, "Well, I'm going to look anyway." To her delight, she found them in the lawn sprinkler, in blowing bubbles, in the ocean and in streams. The children and I decided that finding a rainbow was like being given a gift we didn't expect.

Then the children eagerly gathered around me as I opened my bag of show-and-tell. The first box brought exclamations of joy when they saw the crystal teardrop dangling from a fine fishing line. We held it to the sun as rainbows danced all around the floor, and each child scrambled to catch one as it happily danced beyond their grasp. It was a gift to hang in their window to remember that sometimes the world is not always filled with only good things, but to know that the hard times will pass and the rainbows are our sign of hope that good will come back.

The next surprise gently brought from the bag was a huge prism. When the sun hit this work of art, intense rainbows were reflected on the ceiling and there were more "Ohs" and "Ahs."

One of my grandchildren had given me the next surprise since she knew how much I loved rainbows. It was an electric plug-in machine that projected an artificial arc on the ceiling. This brought forth a lot of laughs.

Had they ever seen a rainbow picture with a pot of gold at the end? Oh, yes they had. The pot of gold came from an old Norse legend.

The people at that time believed that the rainbow was a bridge from the earth to the sky.

I asked the children what they thought might be in that pot of gold. A few replied that they thought it was a present, and one little girl said, "A beautiful day." The most touching remark came from a very small boy with thick-rimmed glasses who said, with a big smile on his face, "The pot of gold is *me* because I like myself!" Everyone agreed that they liked that answer the best.

GIFT OF DISCOVERY

Each season gives us the gift of discovery. When spring approaches, there is a strong call for many of us to get out in the garden. It's almost like waking up from a long winter's nap. Each spring, I dream about what might be under the leaves and the old weeds. Would the garden look different from last year? On a warm sunny day, I take the rake to the soil to find out.

After uprooting several plants with too much gusto, I remember that spring shoots are very fragile, so I change my style to one of quiet, thoughtful raking. I pretend that each green sprout is a very small child. As I uncover the blanket of leaves, I imagine their joy at being able to feel the warm sun on their heads. The rich brown earth will give them strength and stability. The moisture from the heavens will wash them clean.

Could we be like these early shoots? When spring enters our hearts we grow new thoughts and ideas that will need nourishment and care. Our ideas, like the plants, have felt the elements over the winter as we have faced obstacles and problems and sometimes heartbreak, but we survive and enter the days ahead with hope and new vision as we, too, reach for the sun.

Or, let's look at another season. We see the beautiful signs of fall, leaves turning from green to scarlet, yellow, orange, and brown. We feel the cool crispness of the waking hours. Our bodies and minds are invigorated, and there's a new energy in us that wants to rise up from within our depth to shine.

Most of the time we might say, "Isn't that great! I'm glad I had the opportunity to see this in my life."

But wait. There is a higher potential for growth here. Take that quiet time for yourself to go deeper into your being to discover this special gift of the creative self. Your body is like the earth and the seeds you plant inside it can grow and allow you to reap a fantastic harvest. Just like nature, you have this power within you to bring forward new growth in the form of ideas and dreams.

Jamie Sams wrote a fascinating book called *The Thirteen Original Clan Mothers* in which she presents a perfect correlation between the earth and ourselves. She writes that if we transpose the "h" at the end of the word *earth* to the beginning of the word, it spells *heart*.

Reach for the sky and touch your dreams; reach for the earth and touch reality. Mix it all together by bringing into yourself all that you see and feel and hear and smell. Fly like the eagle, letting your ideas and the excitement of discovery flow over you like water to nurture the flower within you. Let that energy fuel the fire inside you as you rise up like the green shoots of spring to face life's challenges.

Our hearts are our gardens of discovery. What will you discover in your heart's garden?

CHAPTER 5

Health

It is our light, not our darkness, that frightens us.

NELSON MANDELA

FEELING SPECIAL
IN A TOO-BUSY WORLD

My daughter said to me, "I feel so overloaded with responsibility and things I don't want to do. I'd like to find ways to feel happy and special." She is not alone in her thoughts. It is a feeling that we all face at certain times in our lives. This happens when the little voice inside of us becomes strong enough to make itself heard: "Let me out! I need care and love! *Look* at *me!*"

When you feel like this, try standing in front of a mirror and look deep into your eyes as you tell yourself, "I care about me. I forgive myself for trying to be a machine. I am a human being, and I need to feel the touch of love. It doesn't always have to be given by someone else; I can give this gift to *me!* Everything will fall into place when I learn to give myself space and realize the necessity of keeping my mind, body, and spirit in balance. I want to be healthy—I have a lot to contribute to life."

I'd like to share with you some suggestions that I received from friends at work. May they help give you a second wind toward feeling special in a too-busy world.

• Buy yourself a fine bottle of wine and flowers on your way home from work and enjoy both while listening to good music. This gives you a chance to quiet your thoughts.

• Try to accomplish the really tough jobs on your task list first so that they are out of the way and the easy ones remain.

• Take your dog for a walk. Enjoy the spontaneity as he explores everything like a child. Exchange lots of affection—hugging, petting, and cuddling—unencumbered by the need for words.

• A good, long soak in an herbal bath at night helps get rid of the day's tensions.

• Enjoy your children or your partner, and do something special with them. Laugh often.

• Listen to energetic music. It will give you a lift and can help elevate your spirits. Turn up the radio as you are driving along and sing at the top of your lungs.

- Treat yourself to a massage.
- Be kind to yourself the way you would be to your best friend.
- Eat well and take your vitamins. Your body is the temple of your spirit.
- Be generous with your hugs. Say "I love you" more often, even if it is to yourself.

- Keep a clear focus on where you are headed.
- Touch nature.
- Give yourself a love pat and listen with your heart more often. Face the light instead of standing in its shadow.
- Smile!

THE GIFT OF LIFE

I'd like to share with you the joy of being alive. I am a winner over cancer, not once but twice. Perhaps you've been in my shoes.

When cancer or any major illness strikes, we are hurt, confused, often angry, and we feel alone. We are told that we need to take one day at a time so that we can focus on gaining back our strength and health. In my own life, as letters, cards, and support arrived from so many people, it was overwhelming to discover that these people really cared about me. I didn't know how they felt up until then. I had been so busy helping other people that I had shut myself off from feelings about me.

One day, as I sat at the kitchen table with an enormous pile of get-well wishes, I took a deep breath and made this affirmation: "I am breathing in all this love and health and as I exhale, out go disease and negative thoughts." I repeated this several times a day, and shortly thereafter I thought to myself, "You know, I am beginning to feel that one day at a time is not enough. I must look farther into the future and make some plans."

I started to take a walk every day and was aware of all the beauty around me. I looked for signs of the seasons changing and heard new birds singing. I filled my thoughts with peace and what was happening at the moment.

On my drives to radiation therapy, I tried to discover something new each day —great cloud formations, the beautiful blue of the sky, sometimes blessing the drip of rain on the car roof, and I searched for interesting people. Each day, I shared what I had experienced with the technicians and smiles lit up many faces. We looked forward to seeing each other.

As I felt health coming back to my whole body, I gave much thought as to why I had become ill. In retrospect I realized that life for me had become a chore. I had lost the spontaneity and excitement for having fun.

I began to think of cancer as not being bad. The illness had been a nudge to let me know that I needed to change my life and that it was up to me to make that happen.

By looking at life with new vision, I rediscovered once more the inquisitiveness of that free child within—always investigating to discover what is new and beautiful.

I urge you to open your arms not only to give but to receive the blessings surrounding you and enjoy the great gift of life!

MUSIC IS HEALING

I discovered the healing power of music by accident. Quite a number of years ago while on vacation, I was rushed to Genesee Hospital in Rochester, New York, with spinal meningitis. My body was wracked with unbelievable pain. By the bed was a small, round speaker radio. By itself, the tone was terrible, but after placing it under my pillow, the music became beautifully mellow. My mind was uplifted and soothed as I accepted the musical flow instead of fighting the pain. It comforted me as my mother's lullabies used to do so many years before.

This healing power of music revealed itself in another way. I have always set for myself the goal of having my garden all planted by Memorial Day weekend. Many times as that date drew near, I planted fast and furious. To add to the problem, my husband, Bob, always brought out the radio for me so that I could listen to the Indy 500 race. Once the race began, my inner clock programmed me to work at the same tempo as the race. By the end of the day, I felt wiped out and always had a huge headache. Then I decided to buy a compact disc player to listen to as I planted the garden. Like a huge wave, music changed the frenzy of a garden deadline to a soft rhythm. By the end of the day, I felt relaxed, and music became my harmonizer.

Music can also become a healing energizer when you dance. Do you notice how you breathe so much deeper as your body is filled to the brim with oxygen? Every organ in your body is nourished!

Have you ever stopped at a traffic light, glanced in your rearview mirror, and caught the person behind you "performing" as a rock star or opera singer? Hearing familiar melodies brings back marvelous memories and can remind you of someone special or of a great vacation you once took. Music lets you slip back in time to relive those days when you felt as if the world were yours. It can become the healing touch of peace and joy.

When my daughter Heidi was searching for a school, we went to Ithaca College. On our tour, we discovered that the symphony orchestra was rehearsing in the auditorium. It sounded beautiful, but the conductor tapped his baton for the music to stop and said, "No, no! It is all wrong. You must get excited! Now let's begin again." The music burst forth with a soul and the tears fell from our eyes. I can never forget this message.

As you go through each day, you need a variety of rhythms changing the tempo like the tides coming in and going out. You need the challenge of new musical sounds to stay on target and make life interesting.

Each of us is like a musical instrument that can play beautiful music. Like the symphony orchestra, we need to continually fine-tune our bodies so that all parts of us play harmoniously together. Let your mind become inspired, your body stretched with energy, and your spirit touched with love. Your music will be the treasured masterpiece of a healthy and happy *you!*

RESILIENCE

One of our employees had always lived on a rented farm. Much to his sadness, it was due to be sold. He said that he had found a place in town and added, "I know I am not going to like it."

"But, George," I said, "You need to look ahead and find a good new path."

He replied, "I can't change." He hasn't moved yet as of this writing, but with support from fellow employees, we'll all help George look at his new change in a more positive way so he can become more resilient.

Think of trees—how they writhe, shake, and bend during a storm. Even ice on the trees forces the branches to bend down, to bow to the earth, but rarely do they break. As the thaw comes, gradually their resilience makes them spring back. Goethe said a long time ago, "We must always change, renew, rejuvenate ourselves; otherwise we harden."

A lesson I learned while raising my children was that instead of being quick to say "No," I should ask myself, "Why not? Possibilities entered my life because I was flexible.

I have a cyclamen plant that blooms profusely and then appears to die. Just as I'm ready to give up and throw it out, it begins new sprouts and comes back to new life.

My daughter was disappointed that roses she sent me for my birthday hadn't held up as she thought they would. I decided to try to revive them. The instructions read that they needed to be submerged up to their necks in warm water and then to have the outer wilted petals removed. Almost all of them came back to life. There was one particular rose that revived sooner than the rest. Its neck stood straight up, its head was the strongest, and it bloomed the longest. I questioned why one would stand out from all the rest even though they were all from the same batch. I guess that roses might be like people. Some have a stronger desire to survive.

A forest fire appears to desecrate the land it burns, leaving it black and devoid of life. Hurricanes and volcanoes wreak terrible destruction, but it has been proven that plant life is more productive following these catastrophes. I have read that sunflowers are being planted near Chernobyl to leach heavy metals out of the soil.

There are stories from all over the world. Native Americans do rain dances to affect plants and prosperity. In India the people use elephants to shake the trees to stimulate growth the following year. In other cultures drum rhythms are used to stimulate nature's production. We prune our trees and pinch the tops of our plants for better growth. The disturbances cause a rise in productivity.

As in nature, it is the disturbances in our lives that force us to be resilient and help us grow in understanding. It is the regeneration force at work.

All elements of nature are part of this life circle. We are all connected. We all need to work together to help the world understand this connection. We are not only caretakers but innovators for the fruition of a healthy planet and healthy people.

In the high triangular window of my sunroom are three wonderful dancing figures. The one on the left is called Celebration. Her dress is glittered with stars as she reaches toward the sky. Her message is, "I value the contributions of all who helped make me who I am now." Touching her hand is a young boy called Turning Point. The last figure, leaping toward the future, is called Rejoice. Her hand reaches back to touch Turning Point's billowing hair. She is calling to him to turn around and come with her as she faces all the new days ahead. Rejoice is a release from the past calling all of us to plant the seeds of new beginnings and nourish them with loving anticipation. Shall we join the dance? She says, "The best is yet to be."

RECOVERY

The operation is over. The reports confirm that I am finally cancer-free! I am writing this on my third day home from the hospital, and it feels peaceful to be here. I'm just so glad to be alive and on the road to recovery.

Yesterday morning I could hardly wait to walk the fields. Excitedly, I made a wish on the first delicious raspberry I picked directly from the vine. Berries taste sweeter when you pick them yourself. I guess the memory of watching the plant develop from the bare winter stalks to the spring leafing and early summer fruition fills the event with high anticipation. I have read that raspberries have a special healing effect in building up the body's immune system.

Positive thoughts from so many friends surround me that sometimes I feel as if I am carried on a pillow of their love. It is a very touching and enriching experience. This gentleness and feeling of wellness is allowing my mind to seek those pools of serenity from pockets of experiences in my life. I hope that I can expand this vision to understand more

fully why I am here and how I can enrich life. What is my purpose, Father Sky, Mother Earth?

As I sit here in my white room filled with rainbows, special art, and memories that are dear to me, there is another new collection expanding. These are sacred stones and healing crystals that have been given to me by special friends.

Before my eyes is a red rock medicine bowl that I found on a hike in Sedona. A high-domed rainbow crystal was given to me as a thank you for helping comfort a couple and ease their pain from the death of their daughter. A lighted crystal was part of a collection from a young man who died from AIDS. He requested that his parents give it to someone who would keep the energy alive.

Several smooth stones once came home with my son David with fond dreams and memories of special beaches and foreign lands. There is a slice of a deep blue geode with a border of white crystals close to its center. It appears to be a doorway to a deeper room that perhaps holds new experience and knowledge.

The last stone is a smaller, nubby geode that somehow has the tendency to stick together even though it has been sliced in half. Each half holds a different core of inner depth and beauty, but the two wells need each other to be complete.

I keep remembering the story called "Blue Boy" by Jean Giono. Toward the end of the story, Opridano, now an old man, speaks to young Pere Jean about life. He says, "Yes, of life. It is that we are only in halves. From the time we began to build houses and cities, since we have invented the wheel, we have not advanced one step towards happiness. We have always been in halves. As long as we invent and progress in mechanical things and not in love, we shall not achieve happiness."

This is what I'm striving for—to look inside life, to tie together the beauty and meaning of it all, and to discover its heartbeat in harmonious rhythm.

My challenge is to help inspire others to circumvent the noise in their own lives so that they, too, can discover for themselves the great mystery of unfolding life within.

How about you?

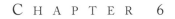

Love

Beauty and Love
These are the priceless things
That feed my hungry soul and give it wings.

THE TOUCH OF LOVE

Can you remember clearly the soft, gentle touch of a tiny baby's hand? As the child grows, he grasps your hand as you tread together on life's many paths. That faith and trust and acceptance is meant to be shared through all of life's passages.

When his life takes a different path from ours, sometimes we forget that special tenderness, and we withdraw our hand from his. The sacredness of each individual life was never meant to be pushed aside, to be left out of the warmth of love.

When our paths appear to separate, we should ask ourselves, "What is going on inside that person that I don't see? Will my gentle touch of holding their hand in care help to heal the hurt of aloneness, alienation, sadness, anger, rebellion? We need not wait until tragedy strikes and find our minds then filled with thoughts like, "If only I had taken the time to reach out."

In our relationships with family, friends, the community, the country, and the world, let's put aside our judgmental thoughts and allow the love and the simple trust we once knew to shine through. Recall the soft tender feeling of that child's hand—the *You* child— and reach out with love!

HEALING YOUR LIFE

There is a wonderful book by Louise Hay called *You Can Heal Your Life.* In the book are exercises to help you heal physically and emotionally, and ways for raising your self-esteem to feel good about who you are.

Hay comments that by the age of three, the fears and acceptances of who you are and how you look at life are pretty well-established. She poses the question, "As an adult, could you go back to the child you were at three and cradle her in your arms to love that child?" I didn't expect my reaction. I was shocked and had a feeling of panic as I asked myself, "What am I going to do with her?" Why didn't I want to pick "Me" up and love her? I struggled for a whole weekend with this reaction.

One morning, as my husband and I were getting ready for work, I told Bob about my struggle and about how hard I had worked on this exercise. I put my arms around him and asked, "Could you have loved the 'Me' child of three?" He laughed and replied, "No way." Sadly, I laughed, too. This filled my mind all morning, and I realized how negative I was being. Seeing the clouds part above me to reveal the azure sky, I realized that the clouds were like my negative thoughts. I needed to look at the clear blue sky inside of me to see what qualities lived there. I made a list.

At the top of my "positive" list was creative and inquisitive followed by spunky and in- novative. That "Me" child had the gift of sur- viving to be someone today who could reach out to touch other people's lives in a meaning- ful way. The list grew as I reflected on all the people who cared about me now. I finally was able to say to myself, "You know, I love that child who had those hidden qualities that no one looked far enough to see at three or four or six or through high school.

I *can* make a positive difference in other people's lives and that has become my mis- sion." Only then could I pick up that little "Me" child and hold her in my arms and tuck her securely in my heart to say, "I love you." The child had come home.

I'll never forget this powerful experience, and I urge you to try this experiment. Hold your "Me" child close to your heart. You are special! Love the unique beauty inside you!

BE A LIGHT

Sitting before me on the desk are two small sculptures of children. The newest is a very young Eskimo child made of pottery. She sits with a beautiful smile lighting her face. Her small arms reach upward to be a receiver of love.

The other represents a slightly older child and is cast from metal. She is part of my childhood and stands on a pedestal called LIFE. Her happy face looks upward, too, as her arms stretch wide. She also appears to be a receiver. The specialness of this sculpture is that she was bathed in some kind of fluorescent coating, and as a child I would often take her into the dark closet to see her glow, fascinated by her ability to shine in the darkness.

In the winter months, when daylight is at its lowest, people complain about being tired and think that, if only there would be more sunlight, they would feel much better. Often they play an impatient waiting game for better days.

Numerous articles appear in magazines and newspapers about what a person can do to get more artificial light to replicate sunlight. We are also aware that our inner emotions can play a major role in our overall health.

On one of these dark days, I got up to take an early morning walk, and with joy I exclaimed that I was seeing a Valentine sky. Crested over the mountain was a deep pink glow. Rising to the heavens like a pinnacle was a bright red-lit radio tower sending its message into our thought waves. It reminded me of a love light. Below this scene were the soft white lights from the town that appeared to be cradled in the arms of the mountain.

Oh, what love can do! It can keep us nourished from the cold, it heals our bodies and minds from negative thoughts and actions, it enables us to reach out to help one another, it's a bond of peace and understanding, and it's a release from pain.

You are like the white lights twinkling in the dark. Reach up to grasp the pinnacle of love light and bring it down to fill your heart. You will find happier and more productive days. You will be filled with energy to share.

So I think about these two precious statues on my desk and the Valentine sky and realize that they have very important messages for us. Instead of being only a receiver of love and light, how about being a giver of love and light as well. If we ignite the spirit of joy within us, it will radiate out to others and at the same time lift us up to have the sun shine from the inside out.

Some of the ways you can be a giver of light are to radiate a smile, give a hug or a compliment, call someone who needs cheer, share a meal and uplifting thoughts, or give a bouquet of greens.

Being a giver of light and a receiver of light is just like breathing out and in. It adds harmony to our daily living that changes lethargy to optimistic energy! *You are light and love* let it shine.

YOU!

Did you ever see the old movie with Robert Young and Dorothy McGuire called *The Enchanted Cottage?* It was one of the most memorable movies that I have ever seen. It's the story of two people who have disfigurements. Society saw only their imperfections, but when they were alone in their "enchanted cottage," they saw only beauty, kindness, and love in each other.

A small child I know discarded a doll because the dog had chewed marks on the foot. How often are people attracted to other people because they are handsome or good athletes or appear to be perfect? Young girls today are being swayed by the fashion industry and TV to present themselves as wisps of thinness as a way to portray themselves as beautiful.

After having a mastectomy, I too had a hard time accepting myself. I was sad and very self-conscious and wouldn't let myself be seen in a bathing suit. I was ashamed of my imperfection.

Another story comes to mind of Albrecht Dürer. He and his friend were struggling young artists, so they decided that one would paint while the other made a living working until they could both support themselves with their artistic talent. The friend worked while Dürer painted. Finally, the day came when it was the friend's turn to paint, but sadly, his artistic hands had become so worn by hard work that he could no longer paint. Albrecht Dürer was so distraught that he painted a portrait of his friend's praying hands. Today, that painting is one of the most famous in the world. It was his gift of love to his friend who had sacrificed so much.

I found a picture showing the inside of the body as a garden and a tapestry of what life experiences might hold. It's almost like a mirror reflecting our inner selves. The caption says, "The irony is, if you don't go in, you can't find out." Do our inner thoughts and actions portray who we are on the outside? Look! What do you see? Do you take the time to look beyond skin to see the beauty shining forth from those you meet? Are we teaching our children to look beyond superficial appearances to the heart of another person? The best things in life don't always come wrapped in a beautiful package.

How you react is through understanding, sensitivity, respect, and courtesy, and then that miracle happens inside of us. The door to our hearts opens and the flame of love reaches out! We can all live in an "enchanted cottage!"

Take the time to go deep inside. Look not only to today, but to all the tomorrows. We are here to make life better for all. It's the dawning of a whole new world.

Greet each day with the salutation, "Good morning life! I hold you in my heart. As I face the day, may acceptance, courtesy, respect, and love be honored as beautiful gifts, and I thank you."

REMEMBERING...FOR
YEVGENI GRINGAUT

It was the week of Palm Sunday, 1990, and Yevgeni had come from Russia to do business with our company. He was a guest in our home. This was a big Russian man with a very kind heart. My husband, Bob, wanted to make his visit memorable, so he asked what special treat he would like to have. To our surprise, Yevgeni told us that he wanted to be baptized in a Lutheran church. He never knew his father but had been told that he had been a member of the church many years before. Yevgeni felt a need to connect with his father now.

At that time of year, everyone was busy. Remembering our children's baptisms, Bob began making a list of arrangements that I would need to handle. There needed to be a community of friends attending, so employees from our company who knew him were invited. Bob insisted that an organist should play soft music for the service and because of the busy season, this was the hardest arrangement to accomplish. At the last moment I found someone willing to play.

I had been caught in a bind that week with too much to do. There were heavy demands at work and with my family, and I wondered if I would survive. I kept sighing and then filling my body with oxygen, hoping that it would release my feeling of exhaustion. Yet under stress there is something in our bodies that gives us that extra energy to do whatever else we are called on to do.

All my frustration melted when I got to the church. A new magical experience unfolded. It was amazing to discover that *three* ministers of the church *wanted* to participate. There was a Russian minister and two from the Lutheran church. The service was conducted in German, and it was truly a celebration of life, of birth, of dreams realized. After the service, the tears rolled down my husband's face as he said, "Do you realize that I am Yevgeni's godfather!"

Our newly baptized friend separated himself from the intimate group. He went to a church pew and with face uplifted, sat alone for a long time in prayer. The beautiful look of ultimate peace on his face told me how much this treasured moment meant to him. I felt humbled. How much we take for granted! He took a risk and made a commitment of faith. My earlier stress and frustration were washed away in the holy water of baptism.

All of us there joined in a spirit of oneness and inward desire to share our friendship with Yevgeni. He represented a coming together of people from a struggling country to know that at the center of all hearts can be found love. At the end of the evening, I thought to myself, "I am truly thankful and await with optimism to be a receiver and giver of whatever else we need to share to accentuate peace and understanding."

Within five months, on September 20, 1990, Yevgeni and my husband were on their way to the airport in Russia when their van was hit head-on by a city bus. They died together.

HEART OF GOLD

I'm sure you have all heard the expression, "That person has a heart of gold." Have you ever stopped to ponder what that means? Is it because someone gives a lot of money to charity? I think there is a deeper meaning than that. What type of person has that kind of heart?

The first idea that comes to mind is a small child. The child knows no prejudices or hate—he emanates purity, smiles, and wonder at the newness of ever-widening experiences.

In my teaching experiences the young children are so willing to try new things. The first several years, "can't" is not part of their vocabulary. Along about third or fourth grade, they often become conditioned by teachers, parents and friends to compare themselves with others, and while book knowledge expands, the child's awareness of his surroundings and his own ability tightens. Thank goodness times are changing and we hear less of expressions such as, "You are not allowed to cry," "You can't do that, you're a girl," "Boys don't cry," or "You'll never amount to anything." As we grow up and face experiences that cause us pain, we internalize them. Hearts harden when we keep that hurt inside.

Think of the correlation of rain and a plant to ourselves. The rains of our lives are challenges, but they give us nourishment. The bud of a flower doesn't resist the rain because nature has programmed it to take the nourishment that will help it unfold into the most beautiful bloom. *We* can bloom by turning life's hard challenges into learning experiences from which we can grow.

To me, a heart of gold is one that has gone through the challenging ovens of experiences and has been purified by rejecting a negative outlook and seeing instead the vast expanding horizons of hope and love.

A heart of gold lives in a person who is striving for understanding and compassion for all mankind. A heart of gold reaches out to others and accepts itself and others for who they are. This allows forgiveness and love to overflow into all walks of life. And then the heart of gold is the quiet, natural self that has become filled with wisdom and harmony and has come full circle from the child bud to full bloom.

Let *your* heart of gold shine on all you touch and fill it with the warmth of the radiant sun.

FORGIVENESS

Many years ago I went to see the movie *Wuthering Heights*. It was a story of jealousy, anger, and revenge. I can't seem to forget one particular scene: As the wind blew fiercely, this young man, so full of rage, slammed the shutters of the huge house and closed and barricaded himself to aloneness.

I wondered what his heart looked like inside and imagined that it was like his house, with dark rooms, damp basements, narrow hallways, cramped spaces, shuttered windows, drawn blinds, and accumulated dust all thriving on his anger. I imagined his tightened chest and rapid breathing as he held on to his negative thoughts and his inability to release the tension he had placed there.

Looking at our own lives, I suspect that we have all gone through periods where we reacted this way. To be healthy, we can't stay like this or we will destroy ourselves from the inside out.

Anger like fire, if held close for too long, burns and consumes the person holding it. How about an annual "forgiveness housecleaning," maybe at New Year's or any other meaningful time of the year for you. At work our word-processing department always has their annual cleanup, in which they close the door to their office and pitch in together to go through all the accumulated paper, asking, "Do we need to keep this?" Wouldn't it be wonderful to do that with all our petty resentments and feuds on a regular basis? It could even become a family activity.

How about making a list of all your grievances. Evaluate each one with the following questions.

• Why am I angry with this person?
• What blame do I bear in this situation?
• Is it worth spending my precious energy

on this resentment? Do I really need it, or could I spend my energy better in another place?

• If I don't need this resentment in my life, why don't I just throw it out now?

For each person you forgive, plant a seed, pull a weed, give a contribution to your church or favorite charity—do something "physical" to symbolize purging it from your life. Then write a note to that person telling him that you forgive him. Whether you send the note or not is up to you—in some cases the person might be long gone or might have moved away. If you have the courage to send the note and let him know that you have resolved the issue in your heart, it could make all the difference in the world and allow him to experience the blessing of forgiveness, too.

For many years I held resentment against my father for treating me as a second-class person. One day, I realized that he did the best that he knew how. I cried, and even though he had died some years before, I said to him, "Daddy, I'm sorry. I wish we could have been better friends. I offer you my forgiveness and love."

Today there are more and more churches

and grieving groups that offer services of reconciliation after a divorce, the loss of a job, or an unexpected death. It is a way to ease the pain and aid our minds and bodies in healing.

One year during the holiday season, I gave to special close friends an antique wine glass with this message.

> *Each antique cup, just like a person, is unique and different. This gift to you is called the "forgiveness cup." Sometimes in our relationships with people close to us, it is hard to resolve conflict. We find it hard to say, "I'm sorry."*
>
> *This "forgiveness cup" is the "bridge over troubled waters." It is for you to use if this happens to you. Please fill the cup with wine and hand it to your friend, signifying, "I give you this gift of forgiveness. May the love lines flow freely between us, the way God created us to be."*

As we insert the key of release into our shuttered hearts, we fling open the doors and windows, light the hearth fires, and let the sunlight flood through to expand our large, airy chambers and widening horizons. The key is called forgiveness and the vehicle is called love.

Nature

*The moment one gives close attention
to anything, even a blade of grass,
it becomes a mysterious, awesome,
indescribably magnificent world in itself.*

HENRY MILLER

COLOR THE SKY GEESE

The weather was unseasonably warm on this particular Monday morning as I drove to the New Farm in Maxatawny, Pennsylvania. The day was an odd one, with everybody anticipating the predicted snowstorm. The sun was only a hazy fuzz ball protruding weakly from behind a bland sky. My eyes were suddenly alerted to a floating black ribbon in the sky. Maybe it was the tail of a kite. My amazing realization was, "Goodness, it's a flock of honking geese fluttering in the sky!"

As I approached the wide open horizon of the New Farm, I exclaimed, "Wow! Fantastic!" The sky became alive with one formation of geese after another. As fast as one flock disappeared over my car, two more bands appeared in the distance. I had never seen anything like this before.

I just had to stop the car. I rolled down the windows to enjoy it all. The call of the Canadian geese was a beautiful sound. I wondered if the honking helped them fly, or if it was only a call to the others to join the crowd.

Gracefully they looped and looped through the sky—sometimes bearing left, sometimes right. It seemed as if this gave the stray birds time to catch up in the flock's pursuit of a colder climate.

I asked myself, "Are there any leaders in a flock of geese?" As I watched, it became evident that they were all—leaders and followers—each one taking his turn. The orchestration of alternating from leading to following had a perfect rhythm that was a real work of art.

How do they know the importance of shared responsibility? How do they know when the time comes to step back and be a follower? What triggers in their minds the knowledge that survival depends on helping one another? It's almost as if they train each other to be winners. Have you ever seen geese fighting each other in the sky? Wouldn't it be exciting in our lives if all the people who surrounded us were nurturers? What would happen in our world if we all decided to bring out the best in each other? Can you imagine the great team we would have living in harmony with each other and the world? The geese can be our teachers if we only listen to the message of their "Honk!"

I had just experienced another momentous day for my book of special days to remember. My eyes opened wider and filled with wonder when I saw nature with its brush, paint the sky—Geese!

LESSONS OF THE FREE CHILD—TIME

It didn't happen according to plan, they had their own fantastic agenda. I share with you two experiences that children taught me about what time can teach us.

I decided to spend about an hour with the day care summer camp program for our company on the family farm to take discovery trips around the fields.

In planning the walks I only thought of finding and tasting herbs, fruits, and vegetables, but the children thought to investigate locust shells, butterflies, grasshoppers, Indian stones, and the sculpture of Fiacre, patron saint of gardens, that had become hidden from view in the overgrown bushes.

"Why is he hiding in there?" they asked. I thought he had just disappeared over the years and never looked to find him.

I became enriched with their smiles and the joy of seeing smudged strawberry faces, the hugs, no thought of time, wandering in wide open spaces where creativity and imagination flourished.

One of our farm staff asked the children if they knew how potatoes grew. It was time to harvest, and as he turned over the soil, the little hands dug fast and furiously to find the hidden treasure trove of potatoes in that earth. "Please can we wash them and eat them now?" they cried.

Little hands were overflowing with tomatoes and yellow banana peppers that could be eaten right then and there, and what a scramble when the everbearing strawberry patch was discovered! "Is this one ready?" was often asked and "Look at this whopper!" As they stooped and searched, it reminded me of an Easter egg hunt. There were squeals of delight, and they ate until I was certain they couldn't eat any more. Finally, my time with them was up and I asked, "Are you ready to go?" Of course, their reply was, "No way! We want to stay here all day and maybe even sleep here!"

Another spring day, I had an experience with three of my grandchildren. I had planned a huge agenda to keep them busy for a good part of the day, but it was like pulling teeth to keep them on my time schedule. Then we went to the mountain.

Joy burst forth as they found new smooth stones in a freshly exposed stream. In the large pond huge frogs huddled together, sunning themselves on the tops of floating pieces of wood, and when we looked more closely, we found tadpoles in abundance. For the first time in the smaller pond, we saw small frogs playing hide-and-seek among the plants growing there as the aroma of spring flowers filled the air.

As each new awareness of nature was discovered in their eyes, the children danced with delight. There were only nature's toys, and time was the least significant thing in the world. Only new joys were important. When I thought the time had come to go, they pleaded to stay, and I only persuaded them by promising to come back soon with lunches and stay for the whole day.

Through these experiences with children, I ask, "Do we take the time to appreciate our children today for their imagination and what they can teach us? Do we take the time in our busy world to quiet our own thoughts enough to listen to their messages and see their beauty? What would we discover if we put our watches away for a day and lived in the moment of new awareness, just as the children do, as nature unfolds before our eyes?

We need to hold on to what is special and important to us. We need to free ourselves to experience these jewels of wonder and then share our stories of what happens.

NIGHT SKIES

I love the night skies! Not too long ago, my dog, Mattie, and I stepped out under the stars. "Star light, star bright. first star I see tonight, I wish I may, I wish I might have the wish I wish tonight." I sighed as I made my wish and sang to myself, "When You Wish Upon a Star." The dark, clear heavens were alive with millions of sparkles. How many wishes could you make to hang one on each star in the sky? Then, I thought about how comforting it felt to think of loved ones no longer with us who have been wafted to the stars and now shine their own light and love down upon us. They are there to help us here on earth.

Throughout the centuries, the stars have been guides for wanderers in the night. Stars were reference points for ships at sea when there were no other visible signs of direction. As I looked at this fantastic spectacle, I realized that there were not only stars but also at least 10 airplanes blinking their lights to signal direction.

I considered then how the light from the Earth looks from Heaven. I remembered flying in an airplane at night and watching how the Earth lights twinkled much brighter than the star lights as the plane came closer to landing. The nearer the Earth, the clearer the light became.

Looking around, I thought, "What about us? We are Earth stars! Like the stars above us, we too can be guides, but sometimes we are like lightning bugs and our lights go out momentarily. How can we be like the stars that shine continually?"

I came back into the warm house and sat down to watch the dying embers in my tiny fireplace, and all of a sudden there was a crackle and a burst of flame. I thought that this is how we are on Earth! To glow continuously, we need a dream to ignite us and help us shine brightly. Holding on to those dreams enables us to inspire our children, ourselves, and all those around us who are looking for ways to climb out of the darkness and into the light.

May we all strive to be like brilliant stars uniting the whole universe in peace, love, and understanding. May light shine on you, fill you, and radiate from you.

A TREASURED EXPERIENCE

The day was particularly changeable. The weather was no exception. I had a deadline for working in my garden in Maxatawny. Could I meet my schedule by finishing before the rain came? The slow drizzle began. All of a sudden, my eyes were surprised by seeing three little children from the neighboring farm slowly making their way down the edge of the cornfield. Nettie and Dorothy, wearing dark babushkas, were leading little Daniel. I asked them where they were going, and they said, "To fish."

Dorothy held a long stick, with Daniel holding on tightly to the other end. I thought that this was to keep Daniel from darting out into the road. As I later discovered, this was Dorothy's fishing rod—not a pole—a board! I called their mother to make sure she knew that the children were going to the pond. Yes, she knew. My fear was that a child would fall in the water, and I was certain that they were nonswimmers.

Hurrying to finish my work, I drove to the pond. Their fresh, smiling faces greeted me as sunshine from Heaven amidst the rain. Leon, their 10-year-old brother, had beaten them there by riding his bicycle. I was amazed at their expertise as they went about their fishing. It was one of the best times of the day. We exchanged wonderful fishing stories. I told them that when I came to the farm I always planned to go fishing, but when I got there I never seemed to have time. I asked myself, "Why?"

Little three-year-old Daniel spoke excitedly in Pennsylvania Dutch. I asked what he said and the interpretation was, "I saw a fish fly!" We talked about imagination and how, to him, it could look like the fish flew as it jumped in the water.

I sat for a long time watching the children fish as the raindrops patterned the pond. I watched five-year-old Dorothy demonstrating her skill using the long board with a string attached.

I thought back to a time when I must have been her age, and my father took me fishing. My rod was a bamboo pole with a string attached. I saw myself in Dorothy. My father and his friends had all the fancy fishing rods, and yet, I was the only one who caught a trout that day. In his excitement my father almost fell in the stream.

I thought all these years that Daddy was excited just because someone had caught a fish. Now I wonder if he was excited because his small daughter with simple tools had made the catch. Was he proud of me? I'll never know. I haven't thought about this experience in a long time, although now it has come back with vivid clarity. I think I could even find that rock I stood on in the stream.

Thinking about life, there is often so much that is left unsaid between people who are close to us. We can't go back for answers, but sharing and encouragement are valued gifts that we *can* give each other *now*. Verbalizing our thoughts is not always easy to do, but it is so much better to take that risk instead of keeping it all bottled up inside.

Reluctantly, I left my little friends by the pond to go back home. With waves and smiles, these peaceful, beautifully radiant Mennonite children who are so close to the land watched me go.

I thought that of all of us, these children were by far the richest.

LATE AUGUST

There is never a newspaper delivered at our farm, so I listen to the good news of life. The birds are busy singing. Bright colors in the garden surround me, filling me with happiness. I watch the collected dew on the tip of a balsam leaf getting ready to drop to the earth. Butterflies and bees are so actively working in the garden at this magical early hour. A gentle breeze blows, bringing refreshment from the heat. I sit here with the last cup of coffee, feeling the peace.

When my husband, Bob, and I bought this farm in 1971, there were no bird sounds and no garden—only parched, dehydrated soil, old buildings, and trees that looked as if time had stood still. I would wake up then to absolute silence. This world has now come alive!

It is here that I've heard the call of the free child to rise up from stress and busyness and enjoy the moment. One evening in late August was a time like that.

I took a walk and, hearing the sound of children's laughter, followed it to the pond. The Mennonite neighbor children were swimming and some were enjoying a great ride in the family's rowboat. The mothers stood knee-high in water holding the hands of the little ones.

Fully dressed, as they were, I joined them. It was a surprise to feel how warm the water was and to feel the delight of the mud squishing between my toes. Can you remember that feeling?

Little Daniel looked very serious as he stood with his mother. This was probably his first encounter with the pond, and I showed him how to splash with his free hand. He laughed and caught on to the fun. The next thing I knew, I was up to my neck in the water, and I was one with them on their evening of letting go. Although my watch was not waterproof, it still ticked on. For this brief time, the schedule clock gave way to the pleasure clock, and it became a reminder of the need to relax and enjoy the little things in life.

Where do we go to find simple pleasures? As we enter the fall season, the changing colors of the beautiful trees are there for our enjoyment. Feel as you quietly stand among the falling leaves, breathe deeply of the frosty air, enjoy the crunch of your footsteps as they make their way across the crispy early morning grass. Hold closely the last remnants of the garden, listen to the music of nature in your heart, and relish the joy of each special moment. As you go to sleep at the end of the day, snuggling under warm, soft covers, light a smile on your face as you remember those simple pleasures!

TREES

When the leaves are beginning to turn, I relish early mornings on our farm. I anticipate the crispness of walking through those leaves as the world takes on a different hue—changing from the green of summer to the fire colors of autumn.

On one particularly beautiful morning, I found a large red leaf, a wonderful leaf dressed in gold, and a green leaf not yet ready to let go of summer. One by one I had picked up this treasured harvest to carry with me. I thought about giving them away, hoping to share the joy I had found in discovering them.

A good friend had just presented me with the gift of a sequoia pine cone. I thought that the huge tree would have a large cone, but instead, it was compact and small and still held a faint aroma of the forest. He told me that he had touched a 2,700-year-old tree on his hiking trip. He had felt the majesty and humbleness of its long life—standing tall and surviving storms, drought, people, and environmental changes. I suggested that the trees could be old storytellers breaching generations of time.

Outside my kitchen window is a huge English walnut tree, the kind that my grandchildren love to climb on among the massive branches and dense foliage. When one of the main branches broke off, I feared losing the tree. The tree surgeon came and pruned out the suckers and reported that the tree would be fine; it just needed the light to reach its center.

As long as a tree lives, it never stops growing, developing stronger roots, and reaching out to seek the light. So if we humans listen carefully, trees can teach us wonderful lessons about the importance of continually growing our roots and expanding our horizons to realize what we can give to each other.

The Native Americans call trees standing people. They believe that, just like humans, trees have strong spirits. In a Russian magazine called *Sputnik,* I read that many people there believe that trees can give you energy and that you can feel their vibrations.

Most every morning throughout the year, I stop under my favorite redwood tree and wrap my arms around its trunk to feel its strength and energy. Sometimes, that energy seems passive, while at other times it seems to rise up through my whole body with extreme vibrancy. I feel the urgency to pass this energy on. I do this by saying affirmations and by expressing my love and care for all the people who are special to me, naming each one. I thank the tree for its strength and love, its beauty and inspiration. It silently shares these gifts with us if we allow them to be part of us.

Sometimes my small granddaughter accompanies me on the walk. I have introduced her to how it feels to hug a tree, too. When she wraps her little arms around the tree, her face looks like the shining sun. I want her to believe that trees are a sacred gift of life.

One fall, the ginkgo tree in my front yard was the source of a wonderful experience. It was a mass of golden leaves. On one particular day after a hard frost, when the air was calm, the leaves fell like raindrops within a matter of hours. I watched the golden pile of yellow leaves grow at the foot of the tree as I worked in my garden. The mailman drove up and with much excitement, exclaimed, "Look at that tree! Isn't it an amazing sight!" I replied, "Looking at all that gold, aren't we rich?" We both laughed.

As the seasons change, please take the time to renew your life's tree. Prune out the bad habits that you don't need anymore. Sometimes it is a painful decision to let go of old patterns that we carry around like those dead branches, but as the sap rises from the roots of the tree, you can make room for the new sprouts of blossoming ideas and dreams. It can be an exciting adventure to let your joyful creativity grow and to feel the warm sun enrich your thoughts.

FREDDIE AND THE DEER

Freddie appeared on the farm a number of years ago. No one remembers where he came from. He is a majestic black and white cat who has respect for people and all his surroundings. Recently, he has gained admittance to 92-year-old Nana's house. Sometimes he sits on her lap or just sits in a position where she can see him.

Nana smiles as she touches his soft fur.

Sometimes Freddie sits outside my kitchen window waiting for food. He wants only the good stuff—nothing with preservatives! He discerns natural cheese from cheese that has additives. He is not a gobbler, but eats with dignity.

One morning very early, he showed me his beautiful soul. Upon rising, I stand in front of the picture window for my exercise routine. I look out among beautiful lawn and trees. On one such morning, five deer meandered into the clearing. They stopped to eat the grass and listen. Under one of the trees sat Freddie. The deer slowly started in the direction of the highway, and, very carefully, Freddie walked over to the lead deer. For a moment they looked at each other and their faces touched for a few seconds. Then, with grace, Freddie took the lead and directed the following deer to the hedgerow—and safety.

How did they communicate to one another? How did Freddie tell the deer that danger lurked in the direction in which they were headed? What instinct or what an unbelievable mind Freddie must have to be able to reach out to Nana in need and to wildlife that to many of us would seem to be his enemies?

As I watch the orchestration of life and animals and all things growing, there is a heightened awareness for how instinct can affect our lives. Notice how pets teach children to communicate love.

Think for a moment how pets can sense our moods. They feel when we are happy or sad or when we are not feeling well. A number of years ago I had a Great Pyrenees dog named Bandit. After I had both my feet operated on, he became my doctor; he insisted on lying on those feet to keep them warm and help speed the healing process.

We, too, sense when our pets are sick and out of sorts as well as when they are happy, but do we fine-tune our instincts to reach out to each other when we are in need of spiritual care? We all have the capability of being sensitive to another's mood. Why wait to be told that we need to reach out when we see the furrowed brow, the sagging corners of a mouth, drooping shoulders, or even a face illuminated with happiness? We are there to lift up or rejoice with one another if we will reach out. Try a touch or warm hug and feel human vibrations transfer like a bridge of love and care.

CHAPTER 8

Quiet Self

I think the tree has taught me more
Than all the things that I adore.
It clings to the earth, yet sees the sky,
And never has it questioned why.

EDWIN LEUBEFREED

HEARTH FIRE

In ancient times February was the month to celebrate the home hearth fire. It represented the return of warmth to the earth. Sometimes, depending on where you live, it can become an impatient wait. Instead of rebelling when nature urges us to slow down, why not step back?

Don't be afraid to take time for yourself. It's time to brighten up inside your life. The winter months can be a wonderful time for inner contemplation. Sometimes we might feel as if we are wrapped in a cocoon of warmth as the earth sleeps quietly. Enjoy these moments of peace.

Here are a few ideas that might help cheer you up when spring seems a long way off.

This can be a time to clear the cobwebs out of your head by cuddling up with a new and challenging book. Books allow us to visit far-off places without ever stepping foot outside our front door. Rediscover the joy you felt as a child when you visited a library and clutched a brand new book in your hands.

Gather warmth and creativity around you.

It's a good time to create a special space within your home that is reserved for quiet time when hectic moments return to your life. Your special sanctuary could be an unused room or just a corner reserved for communication with your spiritual self. It can become a haven where you relax and bring your mind, body, and spirit to its center. Let this space be *your* place to go where you can feel love and warmth.

In my sanctuary—the room where I write— there is a life-size sculpture of an African storyteller. He sat in the center of a village for more than 130 years to remind people how important it was to share their stories so that the tradition could be carried on. Storyteller looks very sad, perhaps because people forgot in the rush of life to carry on their life stories.

In my growing up, February was the month when we worked on updating photo albums as we shared those family stories. We talked about experiences we faced that helped us grow stronger. Never forget how important these family stories can be for the little ones in your life. It gives them a sense of belonging and continuity that will stay with them for years to come.

The kitchen can be the hub of delicious aromas and delights as new recipes are tried. Gather the warmth within your home for your family and friends as you prepare a special meal of old favorite recipes or an ethnic meal. My son said to me one day, "You know, Mom, as long as you have the smells of home, you'll always come back." Good food and good conversation shared with loved ones make an ideal combination when cold winds are rattling the windowpanes.

Valentine's Day must have been placed in February for a very good reason. By rekindling family ties, friendships, and inner spirits, our hearts are building a strong fire of love to break outward into spring!

WAKE UP TO FEELINGS AND DREAMS

As another year or cycle of your life begins, use the quiet moments to create a new you! Think of yourself as a potter who takes the earth, water, fire, and air to mold a beautiful masterpiece. It is you who nourishes the soft, pliable clay in your hands to tenderly mold your masterpiece with love. It is you who are creating your life with dreams to turn into reality.

This a continual process that we often forget when obstacles come into play like divorce, loss of a job, illness, or the death of someone we love. It is then that feelings and dreams can become bottled up by negative emotions stopping our ability to shape our lives creatively.

This happened to me when I faced illness. Life was devastating, and I finally realized that I had to act positively and wake up those feelings and dreams so that I could create a new life filled again with joy. I needed to look inside and take time to regain my center. Then affirmative action helps the body, mind, and soul to heal!

I like to think of the ways we can help ourselves to augment those feelings and dreams. It is like adding the decoration to our masterpiece. Here are some suggestions that can help you.

• Breathe deeply and listen as you draw air in and out of your lungs, giving your body the energy to sweep away negative thoughts.

• Soak in an herbal bath and think about each positive sensation beginning like a drop of water, merging with the stream of your ideas and flowing into your greater self as a river flows into the sea.

• Stoke your inner fire by laughing more

and by affirming your health and energy and feeling good about the special you—a child of God who is able to give and receive love unconditionally.

• Each day write down in a notebook five positive thoughts or feelings that you have. Stretch your horizons and follow each with a statement of a new dream, idea, or challenge to add to your life.

• Take walks, touch the earth, and listen to the silence that surrounds you. Tune in to your own inward music.

• Each day can be the best day of your life. Believe it! Celebrate! Now is the time to wake up with excitement and greet those special feelings and dreams for each new day!

HI HONEY, I'M HOME!

Do you have a secret place just for you? It's a sacred place that waits patiently for you to come still your mind and heal from the cares that are often too much for us.

When I was a small child, our family of six

lived in a small row house, and there was little chance to find a place that was just for me. I found that place in the toy closet underneath the living room steps leading to the second floor.

After I was married and had children, my

secret place was among the trees sitting on the soft, brown carpet of pine needles a short distance from my house. None of my family thought to look for me there. Only Kiki, my dog, would come find me and nuzzle by my side. As I stroked her silky, warm fur coat, calmness became my security blanket from frustration and tiredness at the end of the day. Peace filled me, and I felt renewed energy from my surroundings begin to vibrate through my body.

Some years ago, our family got a second home. It was an old farmhouse that needed a lot of interior work. This became my next retreat where I could step away from the busyness of life to paint and wallpaper, to sit and dream.

Today, when I think of going to this old stone home full of memories from nine generations, the excitement of anticipation mounts. The house sits all alone in the quiet countryside. I open the door and instantly drop the clothes of rushing and too many cares by the doorway as I call out to the majestic silence, "Hi, honey, I'm home!" Like a dear companion, it has been waiting for me to return.

Let your mind be the magic carpet carrying you back to revisit your secret places. If you have lost your special place in today's hectic world, you can find it again or create a new one. There are many places to choose for your hideaway: a park bench, a rocking chair, a porch, a window, a corner of the library, a peaceful church, a garden.

Why take the time to find your own retreat? To allow yourself the privilege of feeling your own uniqueness in quiet time. To treat yourself with love and care in order to nourish your body, mind and spirit. To listen to your own inner voice of wisdom.

The silence is waiting for you to come home to your heart. Your heart's home is a sacred haven filled with peace, joy, and understanding. The warmth of love surrounds you to nourish your soul.

REFLECTIONS
ON WATER

A few years ago, I spent a very special vacation in Oak Creek Canyon, Arizona. My cabin was located in the woods beside a roaring stream. If I closed my eyes, I thought I could be a child again, remembering with longing the mountain retreat our family had in Pennsylvania. The voice of the stream there lulled me to sleep each night, as the stream did on this vacation.

During the day, I spent long hours watching the water tumble over the rocks, creating foam. I wondered where it was running to, and the longer I looked I discovered that there was more to meet the eye than the pounding flow. At some places the rock formation created little pools of serenity where the water was crystal clear. Like a mirror, I could see pebbles at the bottom and the reflection of other rocks and trees. If I looked closer, I could see myself and wondered, if I was quiet enough, would I be able to see my inner soul? These reflecting pools were like little resting places before the energy escalated and the water made its way

through the challenging rock paths. I could see that the water made different paths as it tumbled onward.

All this reminded me of how we face life. I thought about how our lives are mostly like the roaring stream, but to make sure that we are not swept away by its continual flow, we must constantly seek out those little pools of serenity where we can regain the strength to meet and face life's challenges each day.

It was raining. I wanted to walk outside but, because I wasn't prepared for the weather, I stood leaning up against the building, watching the hard-falling raindrops forming puddles on the sidewalk. I watched for a very long time, observing the changes as the raindrops splashed in circles. Sometimes the drops formed big circles that reached out to touch other circles, and they joined together and grew in magnitude and magnificence. Some drops of rain never materialized beyond their tiny circle before they disappeared into oblivion.

As I drew closer to watch this act of

nature, I noticed that colors were added to the reflections in the large raindrop pools. I saw trees and finally was aware of my own image and the images of other people who passed by, and I began to think of ideas as drops of rain.

Sometimes our ideas fall fast in large pools. They connect with other circles in our consciousness and become wider and deeper. They just can't stay there. They need action, connection, and people to grow.

Think about your ideas and how you can enlarge them to join wider circles of influence. Hold them close in specialness and color your ideas with enthusiasm and energy and peace. The spirit of enlightenment and uniqueness is yours to share in beauty with others.

One of my most momentous experiences was on a vacation with my husband in Oaxaca, Mexico, back in the 1970s. We stayed in a very old hotel that had once been a convent. The building wrapped around a courtyard with a pool in the center.

At dinner one particular evening, I wanted to talk but Bob was not very communicative. I couldn't get him moving, and I felt angry. So after dinner I told him, "I'm going down to the pool to see who I can find to talk to." There was no one at the pool, and I thought about our "talk to me" dialogue. To me, conversation is very important because many times it is essential to weigh our thoughts against what someone else is saying in order to test and strengthen our own beliefs. Unless you hold ongoing dialogue with someone, the underground thoughts never surface, and much of that person remains a mystery.

Then I thought how my surroundings were a room with the pool in the center and open to the sky. Somewhere in the background I could hear voices and music, but I was all alone. Looking at the reflection of the surrounding buildings in the pool, I saw unusual arches and intricate doorways that were all the more beautiful in the underwater reflection. It reminded me that inside each of us are doorways that we don't ordinarily see, which are there to be opened and explored—new experiences and new horizons. I'll never forget this revelation for the rest of my life!

CHAPTER 9

Gratitude

To be a human being is an honor,
and we offer thanksgiving for
all the gifts of life.

MOHAWK INDIAN PROVERB

THE ALABASTER
BOWL

Walking through the living room, my eyes rested on a small white alabaster bowl sitting on top of a three-legged amethyst-colored glass stand. I was not aware of the serene white light shining from the center of the bowl before. This was a gift to me from my son. His greeting which was still beside it read, "This small bowl is a symbol of what rests in it from the past and what may fall into it in the future. It is always accessible, so you can always reach your dreams, goals, and memories. Put it in a spot where you can enjoy looking at it often. Enjoy and love looking at life. Lots of love." I picked this glistening bowl up, cupped it in my hands, and thought about its meaning.

To me, the three-legged stool reminded me of the mind, body, and spirit that is necessary in our lives for harmony. The translucent bowl perched on the top of the stand looks as if it is reaching out to be a receiver of good. The perfectly formed rim of the bowl reminds me of the circle of life—no true beginning or end. It regenerates itself like the seasons. The white light is the heart of love that is there for us to share with others. This is a beautiful dream of what life can be for each of us.

What might be some things that we put into the bowl each day?

Memories of loved ones and experiences that helped to make us who we are.

Sensitivity to the needs of others who might need an arm or a hug.

Encouragement that whatever the task is before us, it is possible to find a solution.

Acceptance for who we are. We only need to be in competition with ourselves to be a healthier person.

Respect—acknowledging the need for each one to be their own person even though their point of view might be different from ours.

Thankfulness for the privilege of being alive to enjoy our beautiful world and share happiness with family and friends.

Purpose—what are we living for?

Specialness—we are born the way we are whether it be gay, lesbian, heterosexual. It is not a choice. We are all lovable in God's sight.

Love—the ability to open our hearts wide to bring into our circle people from all parts of the world, to work together, to reach out and care for each other in sickness and health. Love holds no fear.

What a tremendous challenge we have to set an example for our children, for we love them forever.

BURDEN BASKET

Long ago, Native American women carried baskets made of reed and grasses on their backs, which allowed their hands to be free for gathering wood for the village fires or berries and herbs for cooking. Learning what these women did with the baskets when they were not in use fascinated me the most.

The basket was hung outside the door of their living quarters. To them, the home was a sacred place, and so visitors or family members were asked to leave their complaints and problems in the basket before entering. Burden baskets were guardians of the home, and they were reminders to respect the happiness and privacy of each family member. It was considered poor manners to come visiting with all kinds of complaints. The basket was a reminder to each person to reach for their inner strength and the wisdom to find solutions to their own problems.

I was due to go to the hospital for an operation and was feeling very sad. My appointment was set for 1:00 P.M., and I wondered how it was possible to wait all that long time. What would I do? I had just recently read about these burden baskets, so I went to a store specializing in Native American goods to buy one. After hanging it by my doorway, I then "placed" all my anger, sad feelings, and pain in it. Turning my mind around, I then took flowers to a person who needed care and phoned other friends who needed to be lifted up so that, by the time I was ready to leave for the hospital, my spirits were soaring, and I felt as if my battle were already half over.

I thought then about how we all might benefit from the burden basket story. Imagine that backpacks and fanny packs are burden baskets. When you go out for a walk, hike, or bike ride, your packs carry the food and supplies that will sustain you. The pack might be heavy at first, but as you continue your journey, the load becomes lighter.

Instead of negative thoughts, you can fill the pack with happiness and peace as you gather in nature's beauty, the wind, and the sun. You can come back refreshed and hang your pack by the door, emptying all the good and beautiful into your heart to carry with you as you enter the sanctuary of *home!*

My basket has become a very dear friend! It has taught me to trust my own ability and to remember that I only carry those burdens I wish to carry. May the burden basket be a special symbol for you, too!

THE POWER OF GRATITUDE

There are times when we all take life for granted, and then we have an unforgettable experience that draws us back into the feeling of gratitude for the good that comes our way. We need to go back again to express our thankful heart. Here are some examples.

To see the Olympic trials for bicycling and to experience the spectators' participation cheering on the riders was thrilling!

One of the events was the Paralympic, and, suddenly, I looked at the world with new eyes! Competitive cycling is grueling enough, but to see riders compete with only one leg or arm—sometimes without a prosthesis—was beyond my previous comprehension. It was overwhelming to see their determination to overcome difficulties that would have stood in the way of most people. Many of us never set our goals high enough to be winners.

At the end of the competition, I was asked to present the awards. As the recipients came up to the stand, the exalted happiness and emotion on their faces caused the tears to run down my face. Sometimes our tears intermingled as I gave them a hug. In one sense, we became part of each other. I joined them in gratitude for their accomplishment.

I'd like to share a remarkable occurrence. There were many phone calls left on my answering machine from a distressed woman. When I called her back, we realized she had dialed the wrong number. She apologized profusely and told me her nerves were just a mess. I asked her if I could help, and she began to cry. What does a person do in a circumstance like this? I asked her to please go outside and breathe in the fresh air and count all the good things in life that had come her way. Her whole attitude changed! "Oh, thank you so much," she replied, and it was as if a dark cloud had been lifted from her distress.

On one of my travels, I met a man with a wonderful philosophy of living. He told me that for much of his life, he was out to satisfy himself first, and many people he cared about suffered. A series of hard times came upon him, and gradually he changed his outlook on life. He said, "You know, I was always looking for happiness, and I finally realized that happiness was the result of being grateful."

Wake up each morning with your grateful affirmations. See how the power of positiveness spreads through all the cells of your body. Know that each of you has the power to rise up to your full potential. Feel the health and joy of an uplifted spirit knowing that you are loved and can give love in return.

THE EXCITEMENT
OF A CHILD

I was filled with the excitement of a child. The first snow squall came from the sky in a torrent. It was barely possible to see the cars on the highway in front of the house. Beautiful music played on the compact disc player, and in the sunroom, there was a warm fire glowing on the hearth. The snow falling on the skylights made me feel as if stars were rapidly descending from the heavens. I wanted to touch it all.

I could hardly wait to go outside. I lifted my face upward to capture the cool snowflakes on my tongue and cried, "Oh, what a beautiful world. This is all brand-new! It's just like the New Year!"

There is a stirring of new life within us all. It's calling us to new dreams, to think new ideas, to discover new ways to care for families and friends. We need to encourage ourselves to find better ways to keep our bodies healthy and to take care of our world. It is a time to chal-lenge our lives so that we will be filled with all this new energy and appreciation. We need to nurture all these new seeds of thoughts already germinating in our minds.

When other snowstorms are upon us, please ride with them and use this contemplation time to enlarge all your new ideas. The inner creativity needs to grow so large that it is ready to be born in the sun. Look up and out and enjoy each new moment as you capture them like the snowflakes—refreshing, enriching, and loving. They become nuggets of growth in our hearts.

May your days be filled to the brim with new, wonderful surprises, and may we dance in the light of oneness with new joy.

"We give thanks for unknown blessings already on their way."
—Sacred Ritual Chant

TELESCOPIC WONDER

Every day when I wake up, I thank God for the privilege of being alive. My eyes feel as if I am looking through a telescope to see a world full of wonder. I see this world as a gem with many facets. Each new direction I turn to opens up new horizons of awe.

Please turn the scope with me for a clearer vision. We bring into our view not only the world and its beauty, but also we see our families, our relationships, the place where we live and where we work, our community as it expands and then once again we come back to our larger world.

We see not a placid scene, but one filled with action and the opportunity to appreciate and love as well as the challenge for growth and change. We see ourselves healthy and whole with excitement as individuals who each day can make a difference for a better world.

All of a sudden, we see that each of us is a gem with many facets.

We can look at our facets as opportunities through fellowship and care to bring more sparkle to our lives and be a light to help others let their lights shine as well.

Believe that each of you is a unique individual—one of a kind—and realize your tremendous power to reach out and activate your dreams and concerns.

So, keep polishing those facets of you that will add beauty and brilliance to our world. See the amazement that you are capable of, and, as we turn the telescope and focus even more clearly, you will see not only one huge sparkling gem of a world, but you'll see that it is made up of billions of bright shining gems—which are You, and You, and You! Just believe that you can make a difference, and you will! The time is today. Go forward guided by the light of love for all humanity!

A SMILE FILLS
MY HEART

It's just about daylight. Mattie, my Australian sheepdog, nudges me to get out of bed. It's time for our early-morning walk. As I open the door, excitement mounts. The rain has stopped and the air is filled with the aroma of the pine needles and the sound of birds calling to one another. Could they be announcing that they, too, are happy that the rain has finally ceased? A cloudy mist cloaks the back field.

As my boots swish through the grass, chocolate-colored rabbits scurry to get out of our way. We are headed for the raspberry patch, anticipating the beginning of breakfast. Even now at the end of their season the berries are still juicy and sweet. Mattie thinks she is a person too as she pulls the berries off the branches with her teeth. We savor their delicacy, and it tempts us to take more!

We turn toward the hedgerow for our next course—ripe wineberries. These were my late husband, Bob's, favorite. As I pull off the lush red berries, I uncover a little round sphere with protruding tentacles; it is so beautiful, it reminds me of a starburst.

The mist is lifting, and we are almost at the end of the field. Now I can turn around to face the brilliant, rising sun! My whole body is invigorated as we pause to breathe in the glory.

Slowly we begin to descend past the moon garden where the smell of lavender fills the air. We head toward the blueberry patch, and Mattie resumes her breakfast. (She's learned to be selective, pulling off only those berries that are perfectly ripe.) We continue on our walk.

The vegetable garden calls us. Along the way I taste a couple of basil leaves and dill. This morning the green beans are at that very tender stage—what could be better than fresh vegetables right out of the garden? The cherry tomatoes are just the right size—I must have a couple. If all that I enjoyed this morning were arranged on a plate, it would be a real work of art.

We meander past the grapes, noting their development and thinking that this will be another breakfast treat as fall approaches. We walk past the early golden persimmon tree. . .I linger under the branches, remembering. . .this was one of Bob's favorite trees. A smile fills my heart as I think of the fun of our annual contest to see who could find the first ripe fruit.

The day has begun with thankfulness for the fruits of the field, for our beautiful world, and for the joy of sharing our gifts and our lives with one another.

EPILOGUE

I am humbled to tell you about a very special place. It's called the kiva. The seed was planted almost 30 years ago when my husband, Bob, and I began our collection of Native American art. Our first purchases were Navajo rugs. At around the same time, we joined Save the Children so our family could become caregivers to Native American children. Two of those early children are still close to me.

My fascination with the culture of these people grew as we visited Canyon de Chelly and San Ildefonso. Every chance for travel enriched the history and art we were learning about. The spirit of the land and the native people impregnated my soul.

When our company decided to build a large new facility for the book division, we needed a theme, and I knew it would be Southwestern. We worked hard to come up with innovative ideas to let daylight and fresh air enter every office space. Then, I announced that this building needed a heart and in the center would be a kiva. "A *what*?" everyone asked. I simply replied, "a sacred place." The

first day it was finished, the tears rolled down my face. We had accomplished the task.

When you enter the kiva, you can feel the hush. It is a round room in the very center of the building and reflects the sacred structures of the Pueblo Indians. Its simplicity offers solace and tranquillity—a place where you can go to collect your thoughts and bring back peace from a too-busy day. Two Navajo rugs, simple benches, and high wrought-iron candle holders adorn the perimeter of the room.

Suspended from the ceiling is a dream catcher, a handmade webbed circle that is supposed to "catch" bad dreams. As you look up through the ceiling opening in the center, you see a wheel of light. It shines down on a tree stump on which sits a concrete birdbath made many years ago by my son David. In the center of the birdbath is a large crystal that catches the light from above. It is touching to know that our employees—on their own—have placed their gifts of the spirit with a thought or prayer around the base of the crystal.

An amazing story unfolds! One of our employees, Cindy, requested to be married in the kiva. Other employees questioned why anyone would want to be married at work? As I write to you now, I share with you last night's wedding.

The guests entered the candlelit, sand-colored atrium surrounding the kiva. The wedding was a family affair—small, well-behaved boys in suits and ties, little girls in party dresses, parents bearing cradled newborns with little white caps, women in beautiful dresses, and many men sporting pony tails. The guests were seated on white chairs facing the kiva. The entrance to the room was adorned with a white lattice arbor draped with soft white tulle. Soft guitar music played as the service began. Cindy was escorted down the beautiful stairway by her former husband to greet with glowing eyes her new husband-to-be.

Toward the end of the service, the newly wed couple walked to the right of the kiva. On a shelf built into the wall is a Haitian wrought-iron cross. Each partner took a lighted candle from each side of the cross and lit the larger center candle surrounded by flowers placed in front of wrought-iron sculptures of Father Sun and Mother Earth.

At the end of the service, the couple entered the kiva to place their gifts of the spirit in its center as they remembered a departed brother and the love and togetherness of their families and friends. All the while a guitarist played "God Bless Our Love."

One of the guests, who also worked in the building, said afterward, "I am so honored to work here. I have the privilege to walk by the kiva everyday. Sometimes I see people quietly sitting there in meditation. You know, I always feel a special kind of peaceful energy here."

Before going home, I spent some quiet time alone in the now-candlelit sacred kiva. The round room reminded me of a womb—a safe place for our spirits to grow. I thought of the pillars in the room as symbols of nourishment for our spirits and I gave each one a name: Harmony, Compassion, Overcoming Grief, Happiness, Nature, Quiet Self, and Gratitude. They are all finally woven together in a circle with silver and gold threads of LOVE!

LIST OF
PHOTOGRAPHS